DISCOVER HOW YOUR DEEPEST QUESTIONS
CAN LEAD TO LIFE-GIVING FAITH

DEMOLISHING DOUBT

BIBLE STUDY GUIDE
FIVE SESSIONS

CLIFFE AND STUART KNECHTLE

WITH VINCENT ANTONUCCI

Demolishing Doubt Bible Study Guide

Published by HarperChristian Resources, 3950 Sparks Drive SE, Suite 101, Grand Rapids, MI 49546, USA. HarperChristian Resources is a registered trademark of HarperCollins Christian Publishing, Inc.

Requests for information should be sent to customercare@harpercollins.com.

ISBN 978-0-310-17874-3 (softcover)
ISBN 978-0-310-17876-7 (ebook)

HarperChristian Resources titles may be purchased in bulk for church, business, fundraising, or ministry use. For information, please e-mail ResourceSpecialist@ChurchSource.com.

HarperCollins Publishers, Macken House, 39/40 Mayor Street Upper, Dublin 1, D01 C9W8, Ireland (https://www.harpercollins.com).

Art direction: Ron Huizinga
Cover Design: © 2025 HarperCollins Christian Publishing
Interior Design: Rob Williams, InsideOut Design

First Printing March 2026 / Printed in the United States of America

$PrintCode

CONTENTS

SESSION 4: DID JESUS REALLY RISE FROM THE DEAD?

SESSION 5: WHY IS FAITH SO IMPORTANT?

A NOTE FROM CLIFFE & STUART

For those of you who don't know us, we're Cliffe and Stuart Knechtle. We're a father-and-son team from Fairfield County, Connecticut, who, for the past decade, have been traveling to university campuses across the country, hosting open-air discussions with students about life's biggest questions: God, morality, suffering, and the meaning of existence. These conversations are part of a mission that I (Cliffe) started more than forty years ago when I first felt called to engage college students in honest, respectful dialogue about faith.

My journey started with a simple but profound piece of advice from my closest mentor: *Go to where students are, listen to their questions, and engage them with truth and love.* This advice shaped a ministry that has now sparked thoughtful conversations with tens of thousands of students from all walks of life. In 2015, Stuart joined the mission, bringing fresh energy and a knack for connecting with today's generation through social media. Before we knew it, we had fan accounts remixing our videos and were receiving more interview requests than we could handle. People even began to recognize us in public!

At the end of the day, though, we're not looking to achieve social media stardom. It's certainly not why we did this Bible study or wrote the accompanying book. Rather, we want this message to help people understand that doubt isn't something to fear—it's an opportunity for growth. All too often, people feel ashamed of their uncertainties, thinking they're alone in their struggles. But doubt is a natural part of faith. It's a chance to dig deeper, ask hard questions, and discover truth. Over the years, we've seen how facing doubt head-on can lead to profound transformation. It's why we're passionate about helping others navigate their own journeys from disbelief to faith.

In this study, we'll explore the age-old question about God's existence, the reliability of the Gospels as a historical source, the evidence we have about Jesus' identity (and whether it's trustworthy), the critical question of whether Jesus actually *did* rise from the dead, and why faith is so important to our lives. Along the way, we'll share stories, insights, and the lessons we've learned from conversations with truth-seekers. Our hope is that this study will encourage you to embrace your questions, wrestle with your doubts, and ultimately find the hope and purpose that only God can provide. Welcome to the journey.

— CLIFFE & STUART KNECHTLE

HOW TO USE THIS GUIDE

Doubt isn't the enemy of faith but the doorway to a deeper one. If you've ever wrestled with hard questions about God, you're not alone. We live in a culture that dismisses Christianity as irrational, outdated, or naïve. And in that environment, honest questions naturally rise to the surface: Is there credible evidence that God exists? Can you actually trust the Bible? Did Jesus truly claim to be God? Did he really rise from the dead?

These aren't shallow curiosities. They reach to the very core of what it means to follow Christ with both your heart and your mind.

The good news is that Christianity doesn't crumble under scrutiny—it invites it. God isn't intimidated by your questions. He welcomes them. He calls you to seek, to think, and to discover that biblical faith isn't blind optimism but reasonable trust built on solid evidence. As the apostle Peter wrote, "Always be prepared to give an answer to everyone who asks you to give the reason for the hope that you have" (1 Peter 3:15). Faith and reason were never meant to compete. Rather, together they build a confident belief in Christ.

This is the purpose of this study: to demolish doubt—not by ignoring it, but by walking straight through it. You'll explore the evidence for Christianity and be equipped to defend your faith with clarity, confidence, and compassion. Whether you're personally wrestling with uncertainty or helping others navigate their own, you'll discover that Christian faith stands on firm historical and rational ground.

Before you begin, note that there are a few ways you can go through this study. You can experience it with others in a group (such as a Bible study, Sunday school class, or other gathering), or you can go through the content on your own. Either way, the videos are available to view at any time by following the instructions provided with this study guide.

GROUP STUDY

Each of the sessions in this study is divided into two parts: (1) a group study section and (2) a personal study section. The group study section provides a basic framework on how to open your time together, get the most out of the video content, and discuss the key ideas that were presented in the teaching. Each session includes the following:

- **Welcome:** A short opening note about the topic of the session for you to read on your own before you meet as a group.
- **Connect:** A few icebreaker questions to get you and your group members thinking about the topic and interacting with each other.
- **Watch:** An outline of the key points covered in each video teaching along with space for you to take notes as you watch each session.
- **Discuss:** Questions to help you and your group reflect on the teaching material presented and apply it to your lives.
- **Respond:** A short personal exercise to help reinforce the key ideas.
- **Pray:** A place for you to record prayer requests and praises for the week.

If you are doing this study in a group, make sure you have your own copy of the study guide so you can write down your thoughts, responses, and reflections in the space provided—and so you have access to the videos via streaming. You will also want to have a copy of the *Demolishing Doubt* book, as reading it alongside this guide will provide you with deeper insights. (See the notes at the beginning of each group session and personal study section on which chapters of the book you should read before the next group session.)

Finally, keep these points in mind:

- **Facilitation:** If you are doing this study in a group, appoint someone to serve as a facilitator. This person will be responsible for starting the video and keeping track of time during discussions and activities. If you have been chosen for this role, there are some resources in the back of this guide that can help you lead your group through the study.

- **Faithfulness:** Your group is a place where tremendous growth can happen as you reflect on the Bible, ask questions, and learn what God is doing in other people's lives. For this reason, be fully committed and attend each session so you can build trust and rapport with the other members.

- **Friendship:** The goal of any small group is to serve as a place where people can share, learn about God, and build friendships. So seek to make your group a "safe place." Be honest about your thoughts and feelings, but also listen carefully to everyone else's thoughts, feelings, and opinions. Keep anything personal that your group members share in confidence so that you can create a community where people can heal, be challenged, and grow spiritually.

If you are going through this study on your own, read the opening Welcome section and reflect on the questions in the Connect section. Watch the video and use the outline provided to help you take notes. Finally, personalize the questions and exercises in the Discuss and Respond sections. Close by recording any requests you want to pray about during the week.

PERSONAL STUDY

The personal study is for you to work through on your own during the week. Each exercise is designed to help you explore the key ideas you uncovered during your group time and delve into passages of Scripture that will help you apply those principles to your life. Go at your own pace, doing a little each day—or tackle the material all at once. Remember to spend a few moments in silence to listen to whatever God might be saying to you.

Note that if you are doing this study as part of a group, and you are unable to finish (or even start) these personal studies for the week, you should still attend the group time. Be assured that you are still welcome even if you don't have your "homework" done. The group studies and personal studies are intended to help you hear what God wants you to hear and apply what he is saying to your life. So . . . as you go through this study, be listening for him to strengthen your faith, answer your questions, and equip you to share compelling reasons for the hope you have in Christ.

WEEK 1 *at a Glance*

THIS WEEK'S READING	Introduction and chapters 1-2 in *Demolishing Doubt*
GROUP MEETING	Read the Welcome and Connect with the group (page 2) Watch the video and take notes (pages 3-4) Discuss the questions that follow (page 5) Respond to the teaching and Pray (page 6)
PERSONAL STUDIES:	
STUDY 1	"What the Heavens Speak of God" (pages 9-12)
STUDY 2	"Something Cannot Come from Nothing" (pages 13-16)
STUDY 3	"The God-Shaped Hole" (pages 17-20)
STUDY 4	"Design Demands a Designer" (pages 21-24)
STUDY 5	"Right and Wrong Written on the Heart" (pages 25-28)
CATCH UP & READ AHEAD (BEFORE WEEK 2 GROUP MEETING)	Connect with someone in your group Complete any unfinished studies (page 29)
NEXT WEEK'S READING	Chapters 3-6 in *Demolishing Doubt*

SESSION ONE

WHAT IS THE EVIDENCE FOR GOD?

But God made the earth by his power; he founded the world by his wisdom and stretched out the heavens by his understanding.

JEREMIAH 10:12

WELCOME | READ ON YOUR OWN

In 1953, a biochemist named Stanley Miller tried to answer one of humanity's oldest questions: *Can life form on its own?* Inside a few glass flasks, he combined water, methane, ammonia, and hydrogen—gases he believed resembled the earth's early atmosphere. Then he sent electric sparks through the mixture to mimic lightning. Days later, the clear liquid turned pink, then red. When Miller analyzed it, he discovered amino acids—the building blocks of proteins essential for life.[1]

Headlines around the world shouted, "Scientists Create Life!" But Miller knew better. His experiment showed that simple organic molecules could form under the right conditions—not that life could arise from nonlife. Ironically, Miller's work didn't diminish the mystery but deepened it. His success required intelligence, precision, and carefully controlled conditions. What was meant to prove life could emerge without guidance instead highlighted how much guidance was required.

The more we learn about the universe, the clearer this pattern becomes. The laws of physics are fine-tuned with breathtaking accuracy. The constants that permit life are so exact that even a hair's difference would make existence impossible. And the coded complexity of DNA clearly points to a mind capable of writing life's software. The deeper we probe creation, the more clearly it points us to a Creator.

The real question isn't whether evidence for God exists—it's whether we're willing to see it. Some resist because belief feels costly. Others assume science and faith are enemies. Yet many of history's greatest thinkers—from Isaac Newton to Francis Collins—found their discoveries only strengthened their awe of a Creator.

As you begin this study, come with curiosity and courage. Faith in God isn't blind; it's evidence-based trust. Every atom, every equation, every heartbeat whispers the same truth: The universe is not an accident—it's an invitation to know its Author.

CONNECT | 10 MINUTES

If you or any of your group members don't know each other, take a few minutes to introduce yourselves. Then discuss this question:

> On a scale of 1 (low) to 10 (high), what is your interest in the evidence for God and overcoming doubt? Explain your response.

WATCH | 25 MINUTES

Watch the video for this session, which you can access by playing the DVD or through streaming (see the instructions provided with this guide). Below is an outline of the key points covered during the teaching. Record any key concepts that stand out to you.

OUTLINE

I. Cosmological Argument: Existence cannot come from non-existence.

A. Non-existence cannot produce existence; an intelligent creator is more plausible.
B. Chaos cannot produce order; nature reflects an intelligent design.
C. Life cannot originate from non-life; creation requires a source.
D. Human longing for meaning suggests the existence of a transcendent being.

II. Teleological Argument: Order points to an intelligent designer.

A. The second law of thermodynamics suggests a finite universe with a beginning.
B. The complexity of DNA implies the necessity of an intelligent source.
C. Earth's precise conditions for life point to intentional fine-tuning.
D. Science is valuable but limited; omniscience explains ultimate origins.

III. Moral Argument: The existence of objective moral values point to a creator.

A. God's eternal character defines goodness, not cultural or external standards.
B. Objective morality, as shown in history, exists beyond cultural norms.
C. "Our hearts are restless until they rest in [God]."[2]
D. Human value, morality, and belief in miracles point to a reality beyond naturalism.

IV. God vs. Evil Argument: Evil actually points to the existence of God.

A. The existence of evil suggests the need for objective morality.
B. God created a good world but allowed free will, risking rebellion.
C. Jesus Christ offers the ultimate solution to suffering: forgiveness and eternal life.
D. Faith in Christ remains unshaken despite unanswered questions about suffering.

NOTES

DISCUSS | 35 MINUTES

Discuss what you just watched by answering the following questions.

1. Invite someone to read Romans 1:19–20. Paul writes that God's character and power are "clearly seen" through what he has made. How have you personally seen evidence of God's power or creativity in the natural world? In what ways does the beauty or complexity of creation confirm Paul's words?

2. In the video, several arguments (*cosmological*, *teleological*, *moral*, and *existence of evil*) were presented for the existence of God. Which of these connects most deeply with you? What about it feels most convincing or meaningful to your faith?

3. Ask someone to read Isaiah 45:18–19. The Bible's claim is that every galaxy, star, and atom testifies to God's handiwork—and modern science reveals just how precisely the universe is tuned for life. Based on what you learned in the video, how could you have a meaningful conversation with someone who doubted God's existence?

4. There is a deep longing that seems to be built into every human heart—a "God-shaped hole" that people try to fill with other things. What are some common substitutes that people worship today? What happens when those things inevitably fail to fulfill them? How have you seen this play out in your own life or in the lives of others?

5. "Non-existence cannot produce existence." Everything that has a beginning also has a cause—and that cause must exist outside of time, matter, and space. How would you explain this truth to a skeptical friend in simple, relatable terms?

RESPOND | 10 MINUTES

You've just explored some compelling evidence for God's existence—from the origin of the universe, to the design you see in creation, to the universal human longing for meaning, to your own capacity for rational thought. Read the following passage, and then take a few minutes on your own to reflect on how this evidence impacts your faith.

> Now faith is confidence in what we hope for and assurance about what we do not see. This is what the ancients were commended for. By faith we understand that the universe was formed at God's command, so that what is seen was not made out of what was visible.
>
> **HEBREWS 11:1-3**

Faith deals with what can't be measured or proven. It reaches beyond the visible world into God's promises. Why do you think God asks you to trust what you can't see instead of giving you continuous proof? How does this stretch and mature your relationship with him?

The writer of Hebrews describes faith as "confidence in what we hope for and assurance about what we do not see." What do you think that kind of confidence looks like in real life? Where do you sense God inviting you to rest in unseen assurance right now?

PRAY | 10 MINUTES

Close your time in prayer. Thank God for not leaving you without evidence of his existence. Ask him to help you see his handiwork in creation and give you opportunities to share this evidence with those who are searching for it. Pray for those in your life who doubt God's existence to see the Creator revealed in his creation.

SESSION ONE

PERSONAL STUDY

In the group time this week, you examined some of the key arguments for the existence of God. In this week's personal study, you will explore this evidence from different angles. Each study will help you think more deeply about why believing in God is not only reasonable but also why it is supported by powerful evidence from science, philosophy, and human experience. If you are doing this study with a group, be sure to write down your responses to the questions, as you will be given a few minutes to share your insights at the start of the next session. If you are reading *Demolishing Doubt* alongside this study, you may want to first review the introduction and chapters 1–2 of the book.

STUDY 1

What the Heavens Speak of God

Imagine hiking through a remote forest and spotting a phone lying in the dirt. You pick it up, brush off the dust, and marvel at its ability to connect with distant satellites, capture stunning images, and run countless apps inside a circuit board the size of your hand. Would you ever conclude, *This phone assembled itself from sticks and minerals over millions of years*? Of course not. Its precision and purpose clearly point to a designer.

The universe is far more complex than any phone—so finely tuned that even the slightest deviation would unravel everything we know. The "cosmological constant," which controls the universe's expansion, is fine-tuned to an accuracy of one part in 10^{120} (the number 1 with 120 zeros after it).[3] This means that if we were to change that number by just 1, the galaxies, stars, and planets would never form. Life would be impossible.

Earth's position also reveals extraordinary precision. We orbit in the narrow "habitable zone" where water stays liquid and life can thrive. Our moon stabilizes the earth's axial tilt and ocean tides—both of which are essential for the balance of life. Every factor, from atmosphere to rotation, appears intentionally calibrated for human existence.

Some propose a "multiverse theory"—that there are countless universes with different constants, one of which was bound to support life. But that does not resolve the primary questions: *What produces those universes? Why is that process itself so fine-tuned?* Even a multiverse still requires design. As physicist Paul Davies observed, "The impression of design is overwhelming."[4] And Nobel laureate Arno Penzias, who discovered cosmic background radiation, wrote, "The best data we have are exactly what I would have predicted from the five books of Moses, the Psalms, and the Bible as a whole."[5]

When you lift your eyes to the heavens or notice the quiet wonder of your own heartbeat, you're glimpsing the artistry of God. Creation is more than evidence; it's an invitation. Every detail of the universe calls you to worship the One who made it and to trust that your life, too, is part of his beautiful design.

Readings: Genesis 1:1–5; Psalm 33:6–9; Colossians 1:15–17

1. Read Genesis 1:1–5. The Big Bang theory says the universe began 13.8 billion years ago from an extremely dense singularity that expanded into the cosmos. In Genesis 1:3, God creates by speaking: "Let there be light." How does this ancient account align with modern cosmology's idea of a universe that began with a "big bang"?

2. Read Psalm 33:6–9. The author writes that God made the heavens by his word. As you consider the universe's fine-tuning, what new depth does this verse carry for you? What "fear," according to the psalmist, should this create in you?

3. Think of a time when you were awestruck by something you observed in nature (like the Grand Canyon or the Northern Lights). First, describe what you witnessed, and then write down how it pointed you toward God.

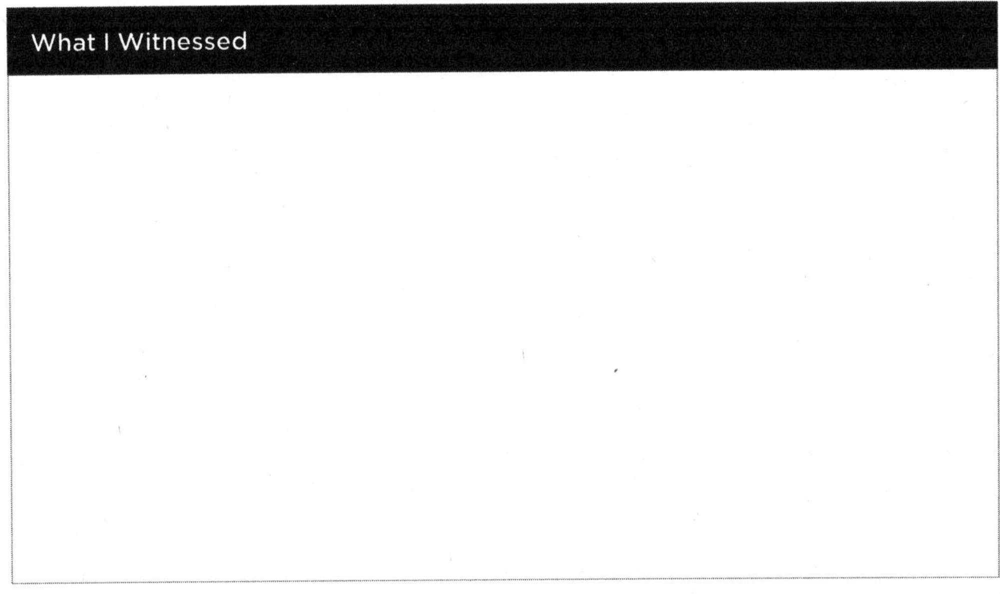

How This Pointed Me Toward God

4. Read Colossians 1:15–17. Paul writes that Christ created and sustains all things. How does this expand your understanding of Jesus?

5. What one piece of fine-tuning evidence could you share this week with someone who believes the universe is a cosmic accident?

STUDY 2

Something Cannot Come from Nothing

In his book *A Universe from Nothing*, physicist Lawrence Krauss argued that the universe could have sprung into existence from nothing. It sounded revolutionary, until philosophers examined his definition of "nothing." It turned out his "nothing" wasn't truly nothing. Instead, it was a quantum vacuum—a restless sea of energy and particles flickering in and out of existence.[6] That's not *nothing; it's something!* This points to a basic truth: Nothing can't produce something. That's not theology; it's logic. Non-being cannot create being.

Scientists once thought the universe had always existed. But then Edwin Hubble discovered the galaxies were racing away from each other, which suggests they were once closer together but then were propelled apart by a powerful event.[7] Later, scientists detected cosmic background radiation—the faint "afterglow" left from that moment of creation.[8] Together, those discoveries made it clear: The universe had a starting point.

The conclusion unsettled many in the scientific community. Even Albert Einstein resisted it. His equations revealed an expanding universe with a definite origin, but he altered them—adding what he called a "fudge factor"—to maintain the idea of a static and eternal cosmos. But when the evidence became undeniable, he admitted his mistake, calling it the greatest blunder of his career.[9]

From this flows what is known as the Kalam cosmological argument: (1) Everything that begins to exist has a cause; (2) the universe began to exist; (3) therefore, the universe has a cause.[10] So, what kind of cause could create the universe? It would have to be:

- Beyond time and space (because it created them);
- Non-physical (because it brought the physical world into existence);
- All-powerful (because it made everything from nothing); and
- Personal (because only a mind can choose to create).

That's exactly the kind of God described in the Bible. Before anything was, God was. Out of his power and love, he chose to create.

Readings: Nehemiah 9:5-6; John 1:1-3; Acts 17:24-25

1. Read Nehemiah 9:5–6. The Levites declared that God made the heavens and gives life to everything on the earth. Why does beginning with God—as the Levites did here—make more sense than believing "something came from nothing"?

2. Read John 1:1–3. John states that all things were made through Christ, who was with God in the beginning. Does that impact how you think about Jesus? If so, in what way?

3. Look at the three premises of the Kalam cosmological argument as given in today's reading. Summarize each premise of the argument in your own words.

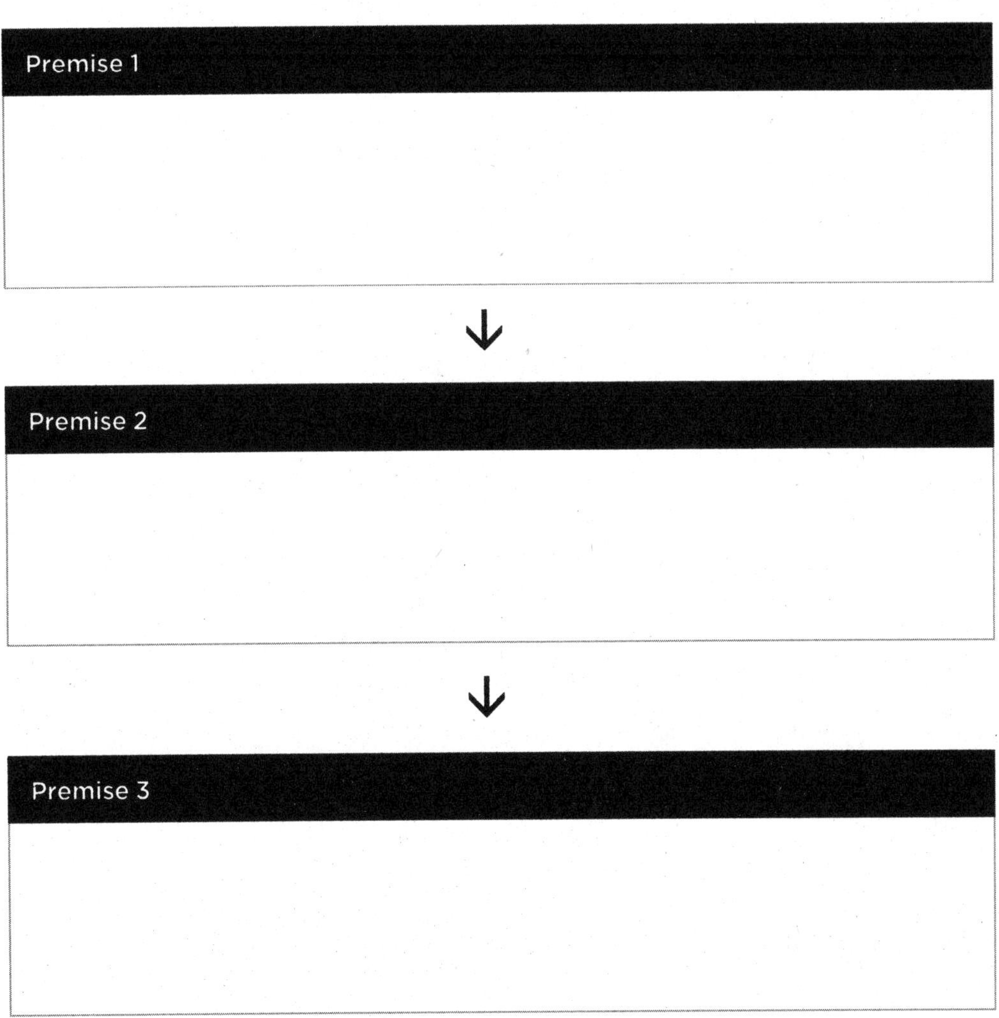

Based on this, how would you explain the Kalam cosmological argument to a friend?

4. Read Acts 17:24–25. Paul says that God "made the world and everything in it." How might God creating the universe out of nothing align with the Big Bang theory?

5. What insights from today's study could help you respond to someone who asks, "What do you believe about where the universe came from?"

STUDY 3

The God-Shaped Hole

Blaise Pascal wrote, "There is a God-shaped vacuum in the heart of each man which cannot be satisfied by any created thing but only by God the Creator."[11] Across every culture and generation, humans share the same ache—a restless longing for something beyond themselves. C. S. Lewis believed this yearning itself is a kind of clue: "If I find in myself a desire which no experience in this world can satisfy, the most probable explanation is that I was made for another world."[12] Our hunger points to food; our thirst points to water. And our longing for deeper meaning points beyond this world—to God himself.

Even modern psychology recognizes the pattern. Across every society, humans are worshipers. We all serve something we consider most important and worthy of devotion. Even those who reject God find themselves devoted to substitute gods: career success, relationships, political causes, fitness, or personal freedom. But these substitutes always disappoint. The career that promised fulfillment leaves you hollow. The relationship meant to complete you falls apart. The body you worked to perfect ages and weakens with time. Nothing limited can satisfy unlimited longing.

This is why Augustine prayed, "You have made us for yourself, O Lord, and our hearts are restless until they rest in you."[13] That restlessness isn't a flaw in our design; it's the point. It's the homing beacon of the soul, pulling us back toward the God who made us. We were created for relationship with him, and nothing else will do.

Even in an age of unprecedented material wealth, rates of anxiety, depression, and suicide continue to rise in wealthy nations. Researchers point to loss of deeper meaning as a primary cause. When people stop believing in God, they don't believe in nothing; they believe in anything. And when those self-made gods crumble, emptiness follows.

What if that emptiness is not an accident but an invitation? What if our deepest desires are signals—arrows pointing us toward home? Our longing for transcendence fits perfectly with the story Scripture tells: that we were made by God and for God. Every restless heart is his reminder that the search doesn't end in success or pleasure or control. It ends in him—and only there do we finally find our rest.

Readings: Ecclesiastes 3:9–14; Psalm 42:1–2; Acts 17:24–28

1. Read Ecclesiastes 3:9–14. Solomon states that God "set eternity in the human heart" (verse 11). Where do you sense this longing for something eternal in your own life?

2. Read Psalm 42:1–2. The author writes that his soul thirsts for God, just as a deer thirsts for water. When have you felt this spiritual thirst? How did you respond?

3. Everyone worships something. Consider some of the "substitute gods" listed in the table below that people worship today. In the empty boxes next to each, write what pull each has on your life and how you might guard against it in your own heart.

Substitute God	Pull in My Life	Guardrails for My Heart
Success/ achievement		
Approval/ popularity		
Security		
Comfort		
Relationships		
Money/ possessions		

4. Read Acts 17:24–28. Paul tells the Athenians that God made people to "reach out for him and find him" (verse 27). How does this shape your understanding of the human longing for transcendence—for something beyond this physical world?

5. God has put eternity in every human heart and designed people to seek him. How could this impact how you share your faith with non-believers? How might you help them connect their inner longings with the God who made them and loves them?

STUDY 4

Design Demands a Designer

In 1859, Charles Darwin published *On the Origin of Species*, in which he proposed that natural selection could explain the diversity of life. Yet Darwin admitted he had a problem. He wrote, "To suppose that the eye . . . could have been formed by natural selection, seems, I freely confess, absurd in the highest possible degree."[14] And this was before scientists understood just how unbelievably complex life truly is.

Biochemist Michael Behe uses the phrase "irreducible complexity" to describe biological systems that only work if all their parts are in place from the start. Take DNA—the microscopic code that carries the blueprint for every living thing. DNA functions like a digital information system, utilizing a four-letter code: A, T, C, and G.[15]

Your body's genetic code contains three billion of those letters—enough to fill thousands of books![16] Where does all that information come from? In every area of life, information points back to intelligence. When archaeologists find ancient writing, for instance, they assume someone wrote it. So when we discover a code far more advanced than anything humans have ever made, why wouldn't we assume a brilliant mind behind it?

Philosopher Antony Flew, once a famous atheist, eventually changed his mind for that very reason. Late in life, he said, "I now believe that the universe was brought into existence by an infinite Intelligence."[17] When we find design, we know there's a designer. When we find beauty, we know there's an artist. And when we look at life itself—the breathtaking order woven through everything—we see the fingerprints of a Creator.

The evidence doesn't just point to intelligence. It points to God, the One who designed life on purpose and with purpose. The same God who spoke galaxies into existence also formed you. You are not an accident. You are part of his design.

Readings: Psalm 139:13-16; Job 38:4-7; Romans 1:18-20

1. Read Psalm 139:13–16. David declares, "I am fearfully and wonderfully made" (verse 14). How does learning about DNA and biological systems expand your interpretation of this verse? How does it deepen your gratitude and worship of God?

2. David marveled at the human body's design and how he had been intricately "knit together" in his mother's womb. In Job 38:4–7, God speaks about the wonder of the universe that he made. Reflect on which aspect of creation most moves you to worship—the intimate or the immense. Mark where you are on this continuum:

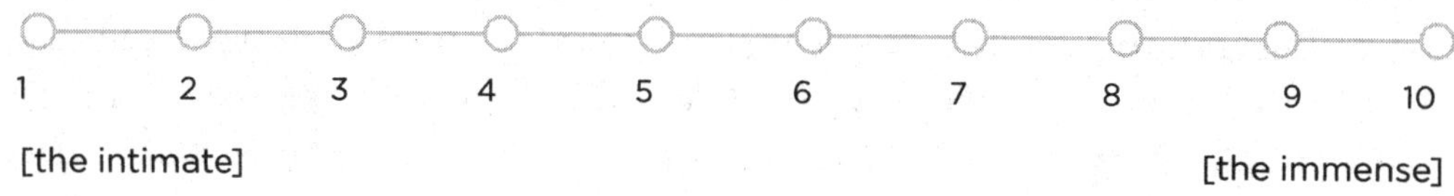

[the intimate] [the immense]

Why does this move you most to worship?

3. Read Romans 1:18–20. Paul says that creation reveals God's "invisible qualities" (verse 20). What specific traits of God—power, creativity, beauty, order—do you most clearly see reflected in nature? Why do you think all of it leaves people "without excuse"?

4. Antony Flew became convinced there was a Creator by evidence of his design. What does his story show about the power of honest inquiry? How might it encourage believers to stay humble, yet confident, when talking about faith?

5. *The same God who spoke galaxies into existence also formed you. You are not an accident. You are part of his design.* Take a moment to consider these statements.

What difference does it make to believe that you were intentionally designed by God?

How might this truth reshape your sense of identity or purpose?

How might it change the way you treat other people?

STUDY 5

Right and Wrong Written on the Heart

After World War II, the world held its breath as Nazi leaders stood trial in Nuremberg. They faced charges of crimes against humanity—mass murder, torture, genocide. Their defense was chillingly simple: *We were just following orders. We obeyed our nation's laws.* Under Nazi rule, their atrocities were sanctioned by the state. But legality doesn't equal morality. If right and wrong are merely cultural preferences, as moral relativism claims, then the Nazis did nothing wrong—they merely adhered to their society's standards.

Something deep within us recoils at that thought. Every moral instinct screams that what they did was evil. This moral outrage points to something higher than human law: a transcendent moral standard. This realization points to what philosophers call the moral argument for God's existence. Every human carries an inner sense of right and wrong—a moral compass that cannot be explained by survival instincts or social convention alone.

If there is no God, there can be no ultimate standard of morality. Right and wrong collapse into personal opinion—one preference over the other, like the choice between chocolate and vanilla. But deep down, we know certain things are *always* wrong, not because society says so, but because they violate something written on the human heart.

Christianity offers a coherent reason: Objective morality flows from the character of a moral Creator. If God exists and has revealed his nature, then there is an unchanging standard by which all actions can be measured. The Nazis weren't just politically misguided or socially cruel; they were morally wrong because they defied the very nature of a holy and loving God. Love is objectively good because *God is love*. Justice matters because *God is just*.

These observations lead to a powerful rationale for God's existence. The moral argument can be summarized simply: (1) If God does not exist, objective moral values do not exist; (2) objective moral values *do* exist; (3) therefore, God exists. Our outrage at evil, longing for justice, and admiration for selfless goodness are not evolutionary accidents but echoes of the divine. They are the fingerprints of a moral Lawgiver who has written his moral law on every human heart—and whose very nature defines what is truly good.

Readings: Exodus 20:1–17; Romans 2:14–15; Matthew 22:37–40

1. The Ten Commandments, found in Exodus 20:1–17, reveal aspects of God's character. Looking at commandments 5–10, how do these specific laws reflect who God is?

Commandment	What It Reveals About God
Honor your father and mother	
Do not commit murder	
Do not commit adultery	
Do not steal	
Do not bear false witness	
Do not covet	

2. Read Romans 2:14–15. Paul writes that even Gentiles show the law is "written on their hearts" (verse 15). How does this "natural law" point to a moral Lawgiver?

3. Think of a recent time when society expressed deep outrage at an injustice. What does that reaction reveal about people's belief in objective right and wrong? If moral values were only personal preferences, how would that change how people respond to injustice or cruelty? How would it change how they respond to sacrificial love?

4. Jesus summed up God's law in Matthew 22:37–40: *Love God* and *love your neighbor.* Why is this a firmer foundation than human opinion? How might this truth guide your decisions in the gray areas where right and wrong feel unclear?

5. Legality does not always equal morality. What is an example that comes to mind of something you saw that was legally *permissible* but clearly *immoral*? How does that tension expose humanity's need for an ultimate moral authority?

Catch Up & Read Ahead

Connect with a fellow group member this week and discuss some of the key insights from this session. Use any of the following prompts to guide your discussion.

- Which of the four arguments for God's existence (cosmological, teleological, anthropological, moral) most resonated with you? What specifically stood out to you about that argument?
- Where have you recently seen God's design reflected in creation? How does considering the wonder of nature move you to reflect on God?
- How has learning about the fine-tuning of the universe and the complexity of DNA likewise affected your view of creation?
- In what ways do you see people today trying to fill the "God-shaped hole" in their lives with substitutes that ultimately disappoint?
- What do you feel most excited to explore in the sessions ahead? Why?

Use this time to complete any of the study and reflection questions from previous days that you weren't able to finish. Make a note below of any revelations you've had and reflect on any growth or personal insights you've gained.

Read chapters 3–6 in *Demolishing Doubt* before the next group gathering. Use the space below to note anything that stands out to you or encourages you.

WEEK 2 *at a Glance*

THIS WEEK'S READING	Chapters 3–6 in *Demolishing Doubt*
GROUP MEETING	**Read the Welcome and Connect with the group (page 32)** **Watch the video and take notes (pages 33–34)** **Discuss the questions that follow (page 35)** **Respond to the teaching and Pray (page 36)**
PERSONAL STUDIES:	
STUDY 1	"Built on Firsthand Truth" (pages 39–42)
STUDY 2	"Guarded by God" (pages 43–46)
STUDY 3	"The Stones Still Speak" (pages 47–50)
STUDY 4	"History's Witnesses to Jesus" (pages 51–54)
STUDY 5	"No Motive to Fabricate" (pages 55–58)
CATCH UP & READ AHEAD (BEFORE WEEK 3 GROUP MEETING)	**Connect with someone in your group** **Complete any unfinished studies (page 59)**
NEXT WEEK'S READING	Chapters 7–8 in *Demolishing Doubt*

SESSION TWO

ARE THE GOSPELS HISTORICALLY RELIABLE?

"Sanctify them by the truth; your word is truth. . . . For them I sanctify myself, that they too may be truly sanctified."

JOHN 17:17, 19

WELCOME | READ ON YOUR OWN

It began with a sound—a rock striking clay. A Bedouin shepherd, searching the cliffs near the Dead Sea for a lost goat, hurled a stone into a cave and heard pottery shatter. That echo led to one of the most astonishing archaeological discoveries in history: the Dead Sea Scrolls. Hidden for nearly two thousand years, these fragile manuscripts contained ancient copies of every Old Testament book except Esther, dating from 250 BC to AD 68.[18]

Before the Dead Sea Scrolls, the oldest complete Hebrew manuscript of the Old Testament dated to around AD 1000—more than one thousand years after most of the original writings. Skeptics had long argued the text must have changed dramatically over time, altered by centuries of copying and recopying, but when scholars compared the Dead Sea Scrolls with those medieval manuscripts, they found the texts were almost identical. Scripture had been preserved with astonishing accuracy.[19]

But other questions remained. What about the New Testament? Can we trust that the Gospels accurately record what Jesus said and did? Were they reliable histories or legends that grew over time? The evidence revealed a remarkable story. The New Testament is the best-documented work from the ancient world. Historians readily accept classical writings with only a few surviving copies made centuries after the originals, but the New Testament has thousands of manuscripts—some within mere decades of the events they describe.

As you explore this session, you'll find that the Gospels are not distant myths or secondhand rumors. Rather, they are eyewitness testimonies written by those who saw and heard firsthand. These are men and women who risked everything, not to invent a story, but to tell the truth about the One who changed their lives—and the world.

CONNECT | 10 MINUTES

Take a few minutes to share anything that spoke to you in last week's personal study. Then discuss this question:

> If someone asked why you trust the Gospels, what would you say?

WATCH | 25 MINUTES

Watch the video for this session. Below is an outline of the key points covered during the teaching. Record any key concepts that stand out to you.

OUTLINE

I. The Gospels are historically reliable, credible, and rooted in evidence.

A. History relies on reliable eyewitness testimony and documented evidence.

B. The manuscript evidence supports the New Testament's historical accuracy.

C. Archaeology verifies Gospel locations like Bethlehem, Nazareth, and Jerusalem.

D. Extra-biblical sources affirm Jesus' existence and the Gospels' historicity.

II. The authorship of the Gospels aligns with historical evidence and context.

A. Gospel authorship aligns with ancient naming and dating practices.

B. Borrowing details reflects shared knowledge, not diminished credibility.

C. Oral tradition and eyewitness accounts strengthened early Gospel records.

D. The Gospels follow ancient biography standards, not historical fiction.

III. The Gospels contain details and human elements that point to authenticity.

A. Manuscript evidence and early quotes confirm reliability and proximity.

B. Unflattering details and human elements reveal authenticity and truthfulness.

C. Thematic event-grouping reflects historical writing, not chronological inaccuracy.

D. The inclusion of "challenging" teachings and the existence of unresolved conflicts highlight the Gospels' genuine nature.

IV. All of the Bible—including the Gospels—is inspired by God.

A. Christians differ on terms such as *inerrancy* and *infallibility.*

B. Thousands of early Christians believed in Jesus without a written Bible.

C. Manuscript variants are minor and do not affect core Gospel truths.

D. Trust in the Gospels stems from trust in Jesus and his teachings.

NOTES

DISCUSS | 35 MINUTES

Discuss what you just watched by answering the following questions.

1. Invite someone to read Luke 1:1–4. Notice that Luke states in his words to Theophilus that he is writing his work "so that you may know the certainty of the things you have been taught" (verse 4). What does this phrase say about God's heart for your *mind* as well as your *soul*? How has God built your confidence in his truth over time?

2. Ask someone to read 2 Peter 1:16–18. Peter insists he wasn't sharing myths but first-hand experiences of Jesus' glory. In your own words, how does an eyewitness account carry more weight than a legend or rumor that has been passed down?

3. The Gospel writers didn't bury the details. They even included the names of people who were alive and could verify what happened (see 1 Corinthians 15:6). If someone were fabricating a story, why would they avoid those kinds of details? How does their inclusion support the claim that the Gospels are historically accurate?

4. Every disciple suffered, and many died, for proclaiming Jesus' teachings and stating that he was the Son of God. What does their willingness to face persecution tell you about their conviction? How does that shape your confidence in their testimony?

5. Both Luke and Peter wrote so future generations could believe with confidence. Who in your life has helped you "know the certainty" (Luke 1:4) of your faith? How can you play that role for someone else? Who in particular comes to mind?

RESPOND | 10 MINUTES

You've looked at powerful evidence that the Gospels are trustworthy—through eyewitness testimony, thousands of preserved manuscripts, and archaeological discoveries that confirm what Scripture records. Take a few quiet moments to reflect on how this evidence strengthens your faith and confidence to engage with those who doubt.

> That which was from the beginning, which we have heard, which we have seen with our eyes, which we have looked at and our hands have touched—this we proclaim concerning the Word of life. The life appeared; we have seen it and testify to it, and we proclaim to you the eternal life, which was with the Father and has appeared to us. We proclaim to you what we have seen and heard, so that you also may have fellowship with us.
>
> **1 JOHN 1:1-3**

John stresses that he personally *saw*, *heard*, and *touched* Jesus. How would this statement have made his readers more confident in the reality of Jesus' life and message?

As you think about all the evidence you've explored today, pause to consider your own confidence in Scripture. How has what you've learned strengthened your trust in the Gospels? How might it equip you to have deeper conversations with skeptics?

PRAY | 10 MINUTES

Close your time in prayer. Praise God for preserving his Word so faithfully and for giving you reasons to trust it with confidence. Ask him to open your eyes to see his presence in the world and to give you opportunities to share this truth with those who are searching. Ask that the Holy Spirit would open people's hearts to see the reality of the living Christ.

SESSION TWO

PERSONAL STUDY

In this week's personal study, you will dig into the evidence for the historical reliability of the Gospels. Each study will help you understand why the New Testament documents are trustworthy and show you how to respond to common objections from critics today. If you are doing this study with a group, write down your responses to the questions, as you will be given a few minutes to share your insights at the next session. If you are reading *Demolishing Doubt* alongside this study, you may want to first review chapters 3–6 of the book.

STUDY 1

Built on Firsthand Truth

Some skeptics argue that the Gospels were written centuries after Jesus' life—long enough for legend to overtake history. But that claim doesn't hold up. The evidence shows the Gospels were composed within the living memory of the events they describe. Eyewitnesses were still alive to confirm—or challenge—what was written in them.

Jesus was crucified AD 30–33.[20] Most biblical scholars date the writing of Mark to the 50s or 60s,[21] Matthew and Luke to the 60s–80s,[22] and John to the 80s–90s.[23] This places the composition of Mark within twenty to thirty years of the crucifixion—well within one generation of that event. Many who saw Jesus teach, heal, and rise from the dead were still alive. They could verify the stories—or expose them as false.

By ancient standards, this is remarkably close to the events being described. The first biographies of Alexander the Great were written more than four hundred years after his death, yet historians treat them as reliable.[24] Even more striking is the context. The Gospels were written in the very place where their claims could be tested. The resurrection wasn't said to happen "long ago in a land far away" but in a specific city, under Roman authority, among real people with real names—Joseph of Arimathea, Pontius Pilate, Caiaphas the high priest. If these details were false, their contemporaries could have easily disproved them. Instead, the Christian movement exploded precisely where these events took place.

The Gospel writers also emphasized their reliance on eyewitnesses. They did not claim to be composing myths or symbolic stories but said they were documenting real events seen by real people. This emphasis runs throughout the New Testament. Paul, writing even before the Gospels, cites specific eyewitnesses of the resurrection—noting that most were still alive (1 Corinthians 15:5–6). His message is clear: *If you doubt me, go ask them yourself.* No one inventing a story would dare invite that level of scrutiny.

The early dating of the Gospels matters because it leaves no room for legends to develop. The authors wrote as careful historians, not distant mythmakers, which is why the early church treasured their words. They weren't preserving legends; they were preserving history—the true story of a man who lived, died, and rose again.

Readings: 2 Timothy 2:1–2; Acts 26:19–26; Luke 1:1–4

1. Read 2 Timothy 2:1–2. Paul instructs Timothy to pass on what he received from reliable witnesses. How does this chain of firsthand testimony—from Jesus' followers to later believers—strengthen your confidence that the gospel message stayed true?

2. Read Acts 26:19–26. When Paul tells Festus "these things" were not "done in a corner" (verse 26), he is reminding the Roman governor that Jesus' ministry and crucifixion were public events. How does this support Paul's claim that what he is saying is "true and reasonable" (verse 25)? Why does the public nature of these events matter?

3. Read Luke 1:1–4. Luke told Theophilus that he was undertaking to "draw up an account" of Jesus' ministry, death, and resurrection so he "may know the certainty of the things [he had] been taught" (verses 1, 4). Theophilus was lacking *certainty* about the Christian teachings he had received and wanted more evidence for his faith. Think about a time you have wrestled with doubt or uncertainty about your faith.

What was the nature of your doubt or uncertainty?

Which piece of evidence from this study so far has helped you address it?

4. There are many people who have never examined the evidence for the Gospels. How will you now respond to a person who claims the stories about Jesus in the Gospels developed from legends? What could you say to that person with confidence about *when* the Gospels were written and *why* they can be seen as reliable?

5. When the Jewish religious leaders commanded Peter and John to stop speaking about Jesus, Peter said to them, "We cannot help speaking about what we have seen and heard" (Acts 4:20). What would it look like for you to have that same kind of motivation and same kind of confidence to boldly share the gospel this week?

STUDY 2

Guarded by God

Historians almost universally accept Julius Caesar's *Gallic Wars*—his account of his military campaigns—as reliable history. Written around 50 BC, it offers Caesar's firsthand account of his military campaigns. Yet the earliest surviving copy we possess of it dates to nearly a thousand years later (around AD 900) and only about ten ancient manuscripts are known to exist.[25] Regardless, no one really doubts that Caesar wrote it.

Compare this to the New Testament, and the differences are staggering. We have over 5,800 Greek manuscripts of the New Testament, more than 10,000 Latin manuscripts, and thousands more in other ancient languages. Some fragments date to within mere decades of the originals. The oldest known piece, a small scrap of John's Gospel known as *P52*, dates to around AD 125—just thirty to forty years after John wrote it. Entire books of the New Testament appear in manuscripts from the second and third centuries.[26]

This enormous body of material is crucial for two reasons. First, it reveals how carefully the early church preserved these writings. They didn't see them as ordinary documents but as sacred truth worth protecting at the cost of their lives. Second, the sheer number of copies allows scholars to spot even the smallest variations. The vast majority of these differences are minor—a missing letter, a swapped word order, an occasional spelling slip. Because of this, scholars can reconstruct the original text with astonishing precision. Renowned scholar Bruce Metzger concluded that the New Testament is about 99.5 percent textually certain—a level of accuracy unmatched by any other ancient work.[27]

Some claim the Bible was corrupted over centuries of copying, but history tells a different story. When the Dead Sea Scrolls—manuscripts from the Old Testament that were a thousand years older than anything previously known—were discovered in 1947, comparisons showed the text had been preserved with remarkable faithfulness.[28] The same meticulous care characterizes how the early church preserved the New Testament.

The Bible stands alone in its preservation, accuracy, and reliability. We have thousands of ancient manuscripts that enable us to trust with confidence that the words we read today were the ones the authors penned thousands of years ago—a message guarded through the centuries so the truth of God's Word could reach us still.

Readings: 2 Timothy 3:14–17; John 20:30–31; Acts 1:1–3

1. Read 2 Timothy 3:14–17. Paul calls Scripture "God-breathed" (verse 16), which means it was written by *humans* under *divine* inspiration. How does this truth connect to the remarkable care with which the early believers preserved and copied these writings?

2. In the fourth century AD, the Roman emperor Diocletian demanded that Christians surrender their sacred books to be burned. The fact that the New Testament exists today is witness to the fact that the Christians of that time risked their very lives to preserve these writings. What does their devotion challenge you to do when it comes to honoring, studying, or sharing God's Word in your own life?

3. Read John 20:30–31. John writes at the end of his Gospel that he chose specific signs to record so "that you may believe that Jesus is the Messiah" (John 20:31). What does this reveal about his goal in writing and the confidence he had in his message? What does John say is the ultimate goal in believing that Jesus is the Son of God?

4. Many believers trust the Bible but rarely think about *why* they trust it. How does learning about the extraordinary preservation of Scripture deepen your appreciation for it? How might it change the way you approach reading it?

5. Read Acts 1:1–3. Luke writes that Jesus gave "many convincing proofs" to his followers "that he was alive" (verse 3). As you close this study, rate how convinced you are that the Bible is reliable, and then write down any doubts that you still have.

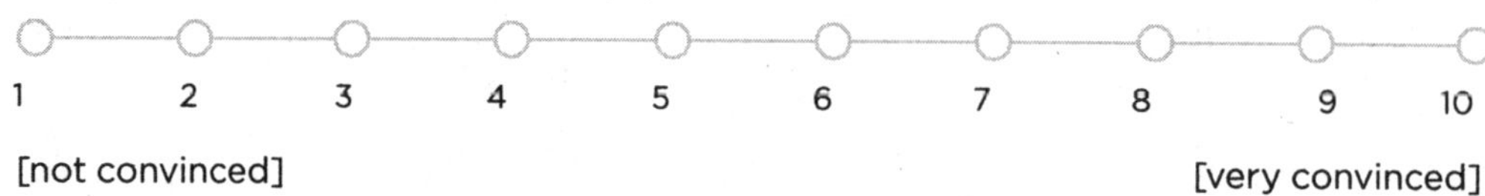

Why did you give yourself this particular rating?

What doubts, if any, do you still have about the Bible's reliability?

STUDY 3

The Stones Still Speak

For decades, scholars dismissed Luke's Gospel as unreliable history. Luke named political figures, official titles, and local details that couldn't be verified, so critics assumed he had simply invented them to make his story sound credible. In the late 1800s, Sir William Ramsay—a well-known skeptic—even set out to disprove Luke's accuracy through archaeological research across Asia Minor (modern-day Turkey). However, after years of excavation and study, he reversed his conclusion. He declared Luke "a historian of the first rank" whose precision could be trusted even in the smallest details.[29]

The evidence backed him up. Luke identified Philippi as a Roman colony and Thessalonica as governed by *politarchs*, a rare title later confirmed by inscriptions. He used the correct terms for magistrates in Philippi (*praetors*) and their attendants (*lictors*).[30] He accurately portrayed the political situation on the island of Cyprus. Details once mocked as mistakes have been confirmed by archaeology and ancient records.

Details in other Gospels have been similarly vindicated. The Pool of Bethesda, mentioned in John 5:1–15, was unearthed in Jerusalem in the late 1800s, complete with the five porticos John describes. The Pool of Siloam, where Jesus healed a blind man in John 9:1–12, was discovered in 2004. Archaeologists have uncovered a first-century fishing boat from the Sea of Galilee that matches Gospel descriptions perfectly, and a stone inscription found in 1961 confirms Pontius Pilate's governorship.[31]

Archaeology, of course, cannot prove that Jesus performed miracles or rose from the dead. But it can confirm the historical framework in which those claims were made. And the evidence shows that the Gospel writers had an intimate knowledge of first-century geography, politics, and culture. They wrote not as distant mythmakers but as those who knew the land, the customs, and the language of their time.

This matters, because people who invent stories about the past inevitably get details wrong. They confuse places, titles, and historical settings—which undermines their credibility. The Gospel writers do not. Their accuracy in the details we can verify strengthens our confidence in the truths we can't—truths that rest not on legend but on history.

Readings: Luke 2:1–2; Acts 10:39–41; John 21:24–25

1. Read Luke 2:1–2. Critics once cited this passage as evidence that Luke's Gospel was inaccurate, as it was held that Quirinius wasn't governor of Syria until AD 6, years after Jesus' birth. However, the archaeological evidence now shows that Quirinius likely served as a Roman administrator *twice*, with the first time being around 7 BC.[32] How does it help you to know that Luke was accurate in even minor details like this one?

2. Read Acts 10:39–41. Certain groups in the first century, such as the Gnostics, believed that Jesus was raised as a purely spiritual being. How does Peter counter this claim in verse 41? Why do you think Luke chose to include this detail in the story?

3. Read John 21:24–25. John insists that his account is based on his own experience. How do you think this personal testimony emboldened his readers to believe that what he was writing about Jesus was true? How might your personal testimony of what Jesus has done in your life likewise serve as a witness to others?

4. Many archaeological finds—from the Pool of Bethesda to the inscription of Pontius Pilate—support the accuracy of the Gospels. Which discovery do you find most convincing? How does knowing that archaeological finds are continually supporting what the Gospels say is true help you with your doubts?

5. The more archaeologists dig, the more truth rises to the surface. What "digging" could you do in your own spiritual life that would bolster your faith?

Bible Study Habits	Prayer Life
One step I can take:	One step I can take:
Fellowship with Other Believers	**Serving Others**
One step I can take:	One step I can take:

STUDY 4

History's Witnesses to Jesus

In the first century, a Jewish historian named Josephus wrote extensively about the history of his people. He had no sympathy for Christianity—he wasn't a believer, nor did he have any reason to promote it. Yet around AD 93, in his work *Antiquities of the Jews*, he made several striking references to Jesus. He described him as "a wise man" who "won over many Jews and Greeks" through his teaching.[33] He noted that Pilate condemned Jesus to death by crucifixion and that his followers "did not cease" their devotion even after his death. He also mentioned "James, the brother of Jesus who was called Christ."[34]

These short references are significant. They confirm, from an entirely independent and non-Christian source, several key facts recorded in the Gospels. Jesus lived, taught, was crucified under Pilate, and had followers who remained loyal after his death.

Later, the Roman historian Tacitus, writing around AD 115, described how Emperor Nero blamed Christians for the great fire of Rome in AD 64. Tacitus, hostile to Christianity, called it a "deadly superstition." Yet even in his contempt, he confirmed what the Gospels report: Christ suffered the "extreme penalty" at the hands of Pontius Pilate.[35]

Around the same time, Pliny the Younger, a Roman governor, wrote to Emperor Trajan seeking guidance on how to deal with Christians in his province. In his letter, dated about AD 112, he described believers gathering before dawn on a set day—Sunday—to sing hymns to Christ "as to a god."[36] His description perfectly aligns with early Christian worship practices found in Acts and the New Testament letters.

Historians call this "enemy attestation"—confirmation from hostile or neutral witnesses. Such evidence carries special weight. When even *opponents* acknowledge core facts, those facts become nearly impossible to dismiss. The early critics of Christianity never denied that Jesus lived, taught, or was crucified—or that his tomb was found empty.

The Gospels, then, do not stand in isolation. Their testimony is reinforced by multiple independent sources—friendly, neutral, and hostile alike.

Readings: Acts 2:14–24; [Tacitus and Pliny the Younger]; Colossians 4:5–6

1. Read Acts 2:14–24. Peter declared to the people of Jerusalem, "Jesus of Nazareth was a man accredited by God to you by miracles, wonders and signs, which God did among you through him, as you yourselves know" (verse 22). How is Peter pointing out that the people *themselves* had been witnesses to the truth that Jesus was the Messiah?

> Nero fastened the guilt and inflicted the most exquisite tortures on a class hated for their abominations, called Christians by the populace. Christus, from whom the name had its origin, suffered the extreme penalty during the reign of Tiberius at the hands of one of our procurators, Pontius Pilatus, and a most mischievous superstition, thus checked for the moment, again broke out not only in Judea, the first source of the evil, but even in Rome, where all things hideous and shameful from every part of the world find their center and become popular.
>
> **TACITUS, *THE ANNALS***

2. Tacitus was a Roman historian and politician. Based on this excerpt, how would you describe his attitude toward the new Christian movement that he was seeing? What evidence does he provide that backs up the Gospels' accounts of Jesus?

> They asserted, however, that the sum and substance of their fault or error had been that they were accustomed to meet on a fixed day before dawn and sing responsively a hymn to Christ as to a god, and to bind themselves by oath, not to some crime, but not to commit fraud, theft, or adultery, not falsify their trust, nor to refuse to return a trust when called upon to do so. When this was over, it was their custom to depart and to assemble again to partake of food—but ordinary and innocent food. Even this, they affirmed, they had ceased to do after my edict by which, in accordance with your instructions, I had forbidden political associations.
>
> **PLINY THE YOUNGER, *THE LETTERS***

3. Pliny the Younger was a Roman governor of Pontus and Bithynia. Based on this excerpt, how would you describe his attitude toward the new Christian movement?

What information does Pliny provide that backs up what Luke, Paul, and others in the New Testament write about Christians partaking of the Lord's Supper?

4. Using the following scale, mark how important it is to you to have sources outside the Bible that confirm events that happened in Jesus' life and in the early church.

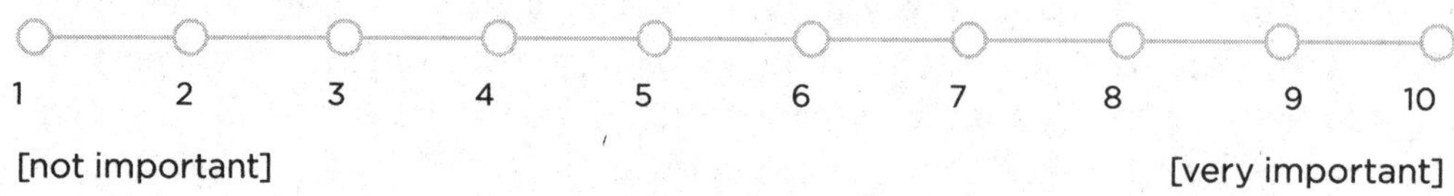

[not important] [very important]

Why did you respond this way?

5. Read Colossians 4:5–6 and think about people in your life who are skeptical or hostile toward the Christian faith. How could you approach them with wisdom and grace this week, showing them that Jesus welcomes their honest questions about him?

STUDY 5

No Motive to Fabricate

People lie for many reasons, but never for one that costs them everything. This is what makes the apostles' willingness to suffer and die for their testimony about Jesus so extraordinary. Their message brought persecution, imprisonment, beatings, and execution. Luke records that James was executed by Herod (Acts 12:2), and there is early evidence that at least Peter, Paul, Thomas, Andrew, and James (the leader of the Jerusalem church) were martyred.[37] Eusebius states that nearly all the apostles died as martyrs for their faith.[38]

It is true that people throughout history have died for beliefs they thought were true—zealots, revolutionaries, religious extremists. But the disciples' case is different. They weren't just believing secondhand reports; they were claiming firsthand knowledge. They didn't die for what they *thought* was true but for what they *knew* was true. And to their final breaths, they insisted they had seen, touched, and spoken with the risen Jesus.

Before the resurrection, these same men were anything but courageous. Peter is famous for three times denying that he knew Christ, but all the disciples fled when Jesus was arrested. Days later, we find them gathered together "with the doors locked for fear of the Jewish leaders" (John 20:19). Contrast this to the stories we read in Acts of the disciples boldly *confronting* the Jewish leaders. Something dramatic had changed. If their message was a lie, at least one of them would have cracked under pressure or confessed to save his life. But none did. They stood firm, even when the cost was torture or death.

The Gospels also contain stories that make the disciples look bad—moments of doubt, failure, fear, insensitivity, pride, and the like. If the writers were inventing stories to gain power or influence . . . why include those embarrassing details about its pillars? Such honest reporting reinforces the truthfulness of the Gospel writers' testimony. They weren't spinning propaganda but simply relating the events as they knew them.

The disciples' transformation demands an explanation. They didn't die for a clever lie or a comforting myth. They died for a truth they had seen with their own eyes: Jesus Christ, once crucified, was alive. Their courage and conviction remains one of history's clearest signs that the resurrection was not a legend but a lived reality.

Readings: Acts 12:1–4; 1 Peter 4:12–16; Mark 10:35–45

1. Read Acts 12:1–4. Luke reports that James was put to death by King Herod. What does this reveal about the disciples' willingness to suffer for their faith in Christ? How does this support the claim they had each radically transformed after the resurrection?

2. Read 1 Peter 4:12–16. How does the apostle describe the situation that Christians were facing because of their faith in Christ? What does this say about the strength of these Christians' beliefs that Jesus was the Messiah and Son of God?

3. We all face moments when holding fast to our beliefs comes at a cost. When have you stood firm for what is right despite pressure? How does that help you relate to the apostles and what they were experiencing due to their belief in Christ?

4. Read Mark 10:35–45. How does this story put the disciples James and John in a bad light? How does the inclusion of this story support the claim that the Gospel writers were not picking and choosing which events to relate to support an agenda?

5. The disciples had every reason to stay quiet . . . but love and truth compelled them to speak out anyway. In the chart below, identify what motivates you to stay silent about your faith at times and what could motivate you to speak boldly like the apostles.

Reasons I Sometimes Stay Silent (Example: Fear of rejection)	Reasons I Want to Speak Boldly (Example: Grateful for what Jesus has done)

Take a moment to reflect on your answers. What would it look like to let your reasons to speak boldly become stronger than your fears this week?

Catch Up & Read Ahead

Connect with a fellow group member this week and discuss some of the key insights from this session. Use any of the following prompts to help guide your discussion.

- Before this study, how confident were you in the historical reliability of the Gospels? How has that confidence changed?
- Which piece of evidence—manuscript evidence, archaeological discoveries, external sources—do you find most compelling?
- How does knowing that the Gospels were written within decades of Jesus' life (not centuries later) strengthen your faith?
- What is the significance of the Gospel writers including "embarrassing" details about the disciples and naming specific eyewitnesses?
- What insight from this session could help you respond to someone who claims the Bible has been corrupted or is unreliable?

Use this time to go back and complete any of the study and reflection questions from previous days that you weren't able to finish. Make a note below of any revelations you've had and reflect on any growth or personal insights you've gained.

Read chapters 7–8 in *Demolishing Doubt* before the next group gathering. Use the space below to note anything that stands out to you or encourages you.

WEEK 3 *at a Glance*

THIS WEEK'S READING	Chapters 7–8 in *Demolishing Doubt*
GROUP MEETING	Read the Welcome and Connect with the group (page 62) Watch the video and take notes (pages 63–64) Discuss the questions that follow (page 65) Respond to the teaching and Pray (page 66)
PERSONAL STUDIES: STUDY 1 STUDY 2 STUDY 3 STUDY 4 STUDY 5	 "Jesus' Claims of Divinity" (pages 69–72) "Liar, Lunatic, or Lord" (pages 73–76) "Fulfilled in Christ" (pages 77–80) "Signs and the Savior" (pages 81–84) "The One Who Stands Alone" (pages 85–88)
CATCH UP & READ AHEAD (BEFORE WEEK 4 GROUP MEETING)	Connect with someone in your group Complete any unfinished studies (page 89)
NEXT WEEK'S READING	Chapter 9 in *Demolishing Doubt*

SESSION THREE

IS THE EVIDENCE ABOUT JESUS TRUSTWORTHY?

The Word became flesh and made his dwelling among us. We have seen his glory, the glory of the one and only Son, who came from the Father, full of grace and truth.

John 1:14

WELCOME | READ ON YOUR OWN

After Soviet cosmonaut Yuri Gagarin became the first human in space, Nikita Khrushchev famously declared, "Gagarin flew into space and didn't see God."[39] The statement was made as part of the Soviet premier's campaign against religion. Gagarin himself, a member of the Russian Orthodox Church, knew, of course, that God is not a physical object hiding in the cosmos, measurable by human instruments or confined to a corner of space.

This is what makes the incarnation so astonishing. The infinite stepped into the finite. The eternal entered time. In Jesus Christ, the invisible became visible. As John wrote, "The Word became flesh and made his dwelling among us" (John 1:14).

But this raises a crucial question: How do we know the Jesus described in the Gospels is who he said he was? Anyone can *claim* to be divine, but what is the evidence that *supports* such an extraordinary claim? This isn't just an intellectual question; it's personal. If Jesus truly is who he said he is, it changes everything. If he isn't, Christianity collapses.

C. S. Lewis framed the issue in his famous "trilemma." Jesus claimed to be God, which means he was either lying, deluded, or telling the truth. There is no safe middle ground for him to be just a "good moral teacher."[40] And Jesus never asked for blind faith. He offered evidence to support his claim—miracles that validated his authority, prophecies he fulfilled, and the ultimate sign: his resurrection from the dead.

Across the centuries, countless skeptics have investigated and found the evidence for Jesus to be overwhelming. Faith in Jesus isn't a leap into darkness; it's a step into light. It's trust grounded not in myth or emotion but in reality. The God who seemed beyond reach came near, took on flesh, and proved himself to be exactly who he claimed to be.

CONNECT | 10 MINUTES

Take a few minutes to share anything that spoke to you in last week's personal study. Then discuss this question:

> What is one claim that Jesus made about himself that you find to be the most compelling or challenging? Explain your response.

WATCH | 25 MINUTES

Watch the video for this session. Below is an outline of the key points covered during the teaching. Record any key concepts that stand out to you.

OUTLINE

I. Historical evidence supports Jesus' existence and the reliability of the Gospels.

A. Manuscript evidence confirms accurate transmission of the eyewitness accounts that are found in the four Gospels.

B. Archaeology validates locations mentioned in Matthew, Mark, Luke, and John.

C. The Gospel accounts were written in close proximity to the events they relate.

D. Matthew, Mark, Luke, and John gained early acceptance among believers in the church as being accurate and truthful.

II. Jesus' life, claims, and miracles affirm his divine identity.

A. Jesus' claims that he was God in the flesh were bold and unmistakable.

B. His sinless life and ethical teachings demand respect.

C. His miracles, like calming storms, were signs of his divine authority.

D. The fact Jesus accepted worship reinforces that he claimed to be God.

III. Faith requires evidence, willingness, and the Holy Spirit's work.

A. Conversion is the Holy Spirit's work and does not come through human effort.

B. Evidence supports belief—but a person must receive that evidence.

C. Human resistance to God more often stems from innate self-centeredness.

D. The cross of Jesus reveals God's love and involvement in human suffering.

IV. Christianity is unique in emphasizing grace over works for salvation.

A. Grace distinguishes Christianity from all other works-based religions.

B. Jesus' sacrifice proves that salvation cannot be earned by human effort.

C. Other religions emphasize merit; Christianity offers unearned forgiveness.

D. It is highly disrespectful to say that all religions are the same!

NOTES

DISCUSS | 35 MINUTES

Discuss what you just watched by answering the following questions.

1. Ask someone to read Exodus 3:14–15 and John 8:56–59. When Jesus says, "Very truly I tell you . . . before Abraham was born, *I am*" (emphasis added), he is deliberately echoing God's name from Exodus. How does this explain why his statement provoked such a strong reaction from his Jewish listeners?

2. Invite someone to read Mark 2:5–12. Jesus heals the paralytic after forgiving his sins. How does this sequence function like evidence validating his claim? If you were in the crowd, what would have convinced you most—the words or the healing? Why?

3. Ask someone to read Mark 10:17–22. This passage is often cited as evidence that Jesus denied his divinity by rejecting that he was good. Notice the man in this story was looking to his good works (keeping the commandments) to inherit eternal life. What was Jesus saying about this kind of "goodness"? How does this shed light on what Jesus was actually saying when he said, "No one is good—except God alone" (verses 18)?

4. Jesus said, "I am the way and the truth and the life" (John 14:6). Why is this claim offensive to many people today? When you consider that salvation is available to *all*, how is Jesus' statement actually *inclusive* rather than *exclusive*?

5. When you think about your own faith, what most convinces you that Jesus is who he said he was—logic, experience, Scripture, evidence, or something else? Why?

RESPOND | 10 MINUTES

You've examined some of Jesus' claims about himself and the evidence supporting those claims. Take a few moments to reflect: If Jesus truly is God in human form, how should that shape the way you live, make decisions, and speak this week?

> "I and the Father are one." Again his Jewish opponents picked up stones to stone him, but Jesus said to them, "I have shown you many good works from the Father. For which of these do you stone me?" "We are not stoning you for any good work," they replied, "but for blasphemy, because you, a mere man, claim to be God."
>
> **JOHN 10:30-33**

Why is clarity about Jesus' identity essential for authentic Christianity? In what situations are you most tempted to soften Jesus' claim that he was God?

How has examining the evidence for Jesus' claims strengthened your confidence in sharing the gospel? What's one sentence you could use this week to begin that conversation?

PRAY | 10 MINUTES

Close your time in prayer. Thank Jesus for not asking for blind faith but for providing compelling evidence for his divinity. Ask him to help you articulate his message clearly and lovingly. Pray for those who struggle with Jesus' exclusive statements, asking that God would compel them to examine the evidence with open hearts and recognize him as Lord.

SESSION THREE

PERSONAL STUDY

In this week's personal study, you will continue to explore Jesus' claims about himself and the evidence supporting those claims. Each study will deepen your understanding of why Jesus, and only Jesus, is uniquely qualified to be humanity's Savior and Lord. If you are doing this study with a group, continue writing down your responses, as you will be given a few minutes to share your insights at the start of the next session. If you are reading *Demolishing Doubt* alongside this study, you may want to review chapters 7–8 of the book.

STUDY 1

Jesus' Claims of Divinity

Some people claim that Jesus never said he was God—that later Christians invented the idea. But this argument falls apart when you actually examine the evidence. Jesus made his divine identity absolutely clear through both direct statements and indirect claims that his Jewish audience immediately recognized as declarations of deity.

Consider his use of "I am." At the burning bush, God told Moses that his name was "I AM WHO I AM" (Exodus 3:14). This divine name became sacred to the Jews—so holy that they wouldn't even speak it aloud. Yet Jesus repeatedly applied it to himself. "Before Abraham was born, I am," he declared (John 8:58). The Jews immediately picked up stones to kill him for blasphemy. They understood exactly what he was claiming.

Jesus accepted worship. Throughout the Bible, we see true prophets and angels consistently rejecting worship and redirecting it to God alone. But when Thomas called Jesus "My Lord and my God," Christ didn't correct him (John 20:28). When a leper worshiped him, he received it (Matthew 8:2). Jesus accepted worship as his rightful due.

Jesus claimed authority to forgive sins. He told a paralyzed man, "Your sins are forgiven," which caused the Jewish religious leaders to retort, "Who can forgive sins but God alone?" (Mark 2:5–7). They understood Jesus was claiming divine authority. His healing of the man proved that he had the power to do what only God could do.

Jesus declared to be the final judge of humanity. He said all judgment had been given to him (John 5:22) and described himself as the one who would separate the "sheep from the goats" at the end of time (Matthew 25:32). He warned that people's eternal destiny depends on their response to him. Such claims make sense only if he were God.

Most remarkably, Jesus said, "I and the Father are one" (John 10:30). The Jews immediately accused him of blasphemy, saying, "You, a mere man, claim to be God" (verse 33). They didn't misunderstand him. They grasped his claim—but rejected it.

Jesus claimed to be God not subtly or ambiguously but clearly and repeatedly. Ninety-eight percent of biblical scholars acknowledge this as historical fact.[41] The real question isn't whether Jesus *claimed* to be God but whether his claim was *true*.

Readings: John 3:1–2; 5:16–23; 20:19–29

1. Read John 3:1–2. Nicodemus acknowledged Jesus as a "rabbi" and a "teacher who has come from God" (verse 2). Most people today are comfortable with acknowledging Jesus as a good teacher. The problem comes with Jesus' claim that he was God in the flesh. Why do you think the second claim is so much harder for people to accept?

2. Read John 5:16–23. When Jesus told the religious leaders, "My Father is always at his work," they "tried all the more to kill him" (verses 17–18). Why did they react so violently to Jesus' words? What did they recognize Jesus was saying about himself?

3. Jesus went on to declare, "Just as the Father raises the dead and gives them life, even so the Son gives life to whom he is pleased to give it" (verse 21). What was Jesus claiming here about his divine authority? What else does Jesus say in verses 22–23 that God the Father had entrusted to him as God the Son?

4. Read John 20:19–29. Jesus displayed his divinity when he appeared before his disciples even though the doors were "locked for fear of the Jewish leaders" (verse 19). What instructions did Jesus then give them in verses 21–23?

Verse	Instruction
Verse 21	
Verse 22	
Verse 23	

What claim was Jesus making about himself by saying the Father had sent him? What authority was he exercising in authorizing the disciples to proclaim God's salvation?

5. When Thomas later encountered Jesus and saw the nail marks in his hands and the spear mark in his side, he declared, "My Lord and my God!" (verse 28). What was Jesus' response to Thomas's declaration that he was God? What does this reveal about Jesus' understanding of himself as the divine Son of God?

STUDY 2

Liar, Lunatic, or Lord

C. S. Lewis famously wrote, "I am trying here to prevent anyone saying the really foolish thing that people often say about Him: 'I'm ready to accept Jesus as a great moral teacher, but I don't accept his claim to be God.' That is the one thing we must not say. A man who was merely a man and said the sort of things Jesus said would not be a great moral teacher. He would either be a lunatic—on the level with the man who says he is a poached egg—or else he would be the Devil of Hell. You must make your choice."[42]

Jesus either misled people about his identity (making him a *liar*), genuinely believed that he was God but was mistaken (making him a *lunatic*), or accurately claimed that he was God in the flesh (making him *Lord*). There is no middle ground.

Was Jesus a liar? This seems implausible. Liars lie for personal gain—money, power, pleasure, or safety. But Jesus' claims brought him poverty, opposition, and ultimately crucifixion. Moreover, Jesus' teachings emphasize honesty and integrity, and his life demonstrated remarkable moral consistency. Would a deceiver invent teachings like the Sermon on the Mount? Would a fraud willingly die rather than admit the truth?

Was Jesus a lunatic? This also seems unlikely. Those who suffer from delusions of grandeur typically show other signs of mental instability—erratic behavior, disconnection from reality, inability to function in relationships. Yet Jesus displayed profound wisdom that still astonishes us today, emotional stability even under pressure, and remarkable insight into human nature. His interactions showed deep empathy and understanding. Even Jesus' opponents, the Jewish religious leaders, never suggested he was insane.

Was Jesus the Lord? This is the only reasonable option that remains. What Jesus said about himself was absolutely true. He was God come in human flesh. The evidence supports this conclusion. His miracles validated his claims. His fulfilled prophecies demonstrated his divine knowledge. His resurrection from the dead proved his power over death itself. His transformed disciples testified to encountering him alive.

Paul, writing before the Gospels appeared, claimed that every person will one day "acknowledge that Jesus Christ is Lord" (Philippians 2:11). This was the consistent testimony of the early church—not something made up later by the Christians who came after. The New Testament is clear that Jesus not only *claimed* to be God but *was* God.

Readings: Mark 2:1–12; 3:20–29; Philippians 2:5–11

1. Read Mark 2:1–12. The teachers of the law accused Jesus (in their minds) of blasphemy—of making claims about himself that were lies. How did Jesus demonstrate that he was telling the truth and did have the authority to forgive sins?

2. Read Mark 3:20–29. This story shows the responses of two separate groups to Jesus' claims of divinity. Name each group and write down what they said about Jesus.

Verse	Group	Statement About Jesus
Verse 21		
Verse 22		

How did Jesus respond to these accusations in verses 23–29?

3. Read Philippians 2:5–11. What does Paul say about Jesus? What does this reveal about the early church's understanding of who Jesus claimed to be—and who he was?

4. Jesus' claims of being God lead to only three conclusions: (1) He was intentionally deceiving people, (2) he was deluded, or (3) he was divine. What have you learned in this lesson that helps you respond to people who say Jesus was a liar or a lunatic?

5. If you accept that Jesus truly is Lord, what impact should that have on you? What is one area of your life that needs to come under his authority right now?

STUDY 3

Fulfilled in Christ

Mathematician Peter Stoner once calculated the probability of one person accidentally fulfilling just eight Old Testament prophecies about the Messiah. His conclusion: 1 in 100,000,000,000,000,000. To explain this probability, Stoner asked people to imagine the state of Texas covered two feet deep in silver dollars. Mark one coin, blindfold someone, and ask that person to walk anywhere across Texas and pick up that one marked coin on their first try. That is the probability of fulfilling just eight prophecies by chance.[43]

But Jesus didn't fulfill just *eight* prophecies. He fulfilled *dozens* of specific predictions written centuries before his birth. The prophet Micah, writing around 700 BC, predicted the Messiah would be born in Bethlehem—a tiny, insignificant village (Micah 5:2). Zechariah predicted he would enter Jerusalem riding on a donkey (Zechariah 9:9). Isaiah described his suffering and death with stunning precision (Isaiah 53:1–12)—and his account was written seven hundred years before crucifixion was even invented as a method of execution.

Some skeptics claim that Jesus arranged his life to fulfill prophecies. But Jesus couldn't control where he was born, his family lineage, the method of his execution, or that soldiers would gamble for his clothing. He couldn't stage his betrayal for exactly thirty pieces of silver or arrange for his side to be pierced while his legs remained unbroken.

Jesus' fulfillment of Old Testament prophecy is important because it demonstrates *divine* orchestration. Only God knows "the end from the beginning" with certainty (Isaiah 46:10). When he announces specific details centuries in advance, and they come true exactly as predicted, it validates both the prophetic message and the One fulfilling it.

Jesus himself pointed to fulfilled prophecy as evidence of his identity. After his resurrection, he told two of his followers who were on the road to Emmaus, "This is what I told you while I was still with you: Everything must be fulfilled that is written about me in the Law of Moses, the Prophets and the Psalms" (Luke 24:44). Jesus expected his followers to examine the evidence and draw reasonable conclusions.

The prophecies that Jesus fulfilled are not vague predictions that could apply to anyone. They are specific, detailed, and verifiable. Together, they form a divine fingerprint that unmistakably identifies Jesus as the promised Messiah.

Readings: Micah 5:2; Matthew 2:1–6; Zechariah 9:9–13; Isaiah 53:1–12; Luke 24:13–35

1. Read Micah 5:2. The prophet foretold the Messiah would be born in Bethlehem—a tiny, insignificant, unlikely place for the "ruler over Israel" to be born. According to Matthew 2:1–6, how did this prophecy come true? How does this detail strengthen the case that God orchestrated Jesus' story and that he was the Messiah?

2. Zechariah foretold the Messiah would enter into Jerusalem riding on a lowly donkey. When you consider Zechariah 9:9–13, what statement was Jesus making about himself when he fulfilled this prophecy by making his triumphal entry into Jerusalem riding on a donkey? What was Jesus saying about the kind of kingdom that he was bringing?

3. Isaiah 53:1–12 contains many details about the Messiah that were fulfilled in Christ. In the table below, write out how Jesus fulfilled each of the prophecies mentioned.

Isaiah's Prophecy	Fulfillment in Christ
Despised and rejected (verse 3)	Matthew 13:53–58
Pierced for our transgressions (verse 5)	John 19:33–34
Oppressed and afflicted, yet silent (verse 7)	Mark 14:60–61
Buried with the rich in his death (verse 9)	Mark 15:42–46

4. Read Luke 24:13–35. The resurrected Jesus here speaks with two of his followers on the road to Emmaus. Jesus tells them that everything written about him had to be fulfilled, tying his life to the entire biblical story. What does this teach you about Jesus' understanding of his own mission? How does it shape your view of the Bible's unity?

5. Fulfilled prophecy shows that God always keeps his word. How does that truth encourage you to trust him with your unanswered prayers or uncertain future?

STUDY 4

Signs and the Savior

Imagine standing in a crowd as a man touches a leper and the disease instantly disappears. You watch him speak to a raging storm and the wind obeys. You see him call into a tomb and a dead man walks out. You realize *these are divine fingerprints.* Jesus' miracles weren't about impressing people or even relieving pain—though his compassion was undeniable. John's Gospel calls them *signs* because they pointed beyond the miracle itself to the Miracle Worker. Each one revealed who Jesus truly was—God in human form.

When Jesus saw the faith of the friends of a paralyzed man, he first said, "Friend, your sins are forgiven" (Luke 5:20). The religious leaders erupted—this was blasphemy! So Jesus gave them a *sign* that he had the authority to forgive sins. "He said to the paralyzed man, 'I tell you, get up, take your mat and go home.' Immediately he stood up in front of them" (verses 24–25). The miracle was evidence that Jesus' authority was divine.

Jesus performed many other such signs. He commanded the natural world: stilling storms, walking on water, multiplying bread and fish. He ruled over sickness: cleansing lepers, restoring sight, and making the lame leap for joy. He even conquered death itself—raising Jairus's daughter (Luke 8:54–55), the widow's son at Nain (Luke 7:14–15), and Lazarus, who had been buried four days (John 11:43–44).

These were public acts witnessed by crowds—including skeptics determined to discredit him. In fact, one time when Jesus healed a man born blind, the religious leaders launched a full investigation. They interrogated the man, questioned his parents, and tried to explain it away. But the evidence was undeniable. The healed man's own testimony was this: "Whether he is a sinner or not, I don't know. One thing I do know. I was blind but now I see!" (John 9:25). Their only solution was to expel the healed man from the synagogue.

John ends his gospel this way: "Jesus performed many other signs in the presence of his disciples, which are not recorded in this book. But these are written that you may believe that Jesus is the Messiah, the Son of God" (John 20:30–31). The miracles were never random acts of kindness. They were flashing arrows pointing straight to his divine identity—the unmistakable proof that God had been made flesh.

Readings: John 2:1–11; 11:38–44; Mark 4:35–41; 5:1–43; 6:30–44; 8:22–25

1. Read John 2:1–11. At the wedding in Cana, Jesus turned water into wine—the first of his signs—even though he said, "My hour has not yet come" (verse 4). Why do you think Jesus did this miracle even though the time had not yet come for him to reveal himself as the Messiah? What impact did the sign have on those who witnessed it?

2. Read John 11:38–44. Jesus raised Lazarus after he had been dead for four days. In Jewish belief, the soul lingered near the body for three days and would only depart completely on the fourth day.[44] How does this background information, and the timing of Jesus' miracle, provide even more convincing evidence that his power was divine?

3. Each of Jesus' miracles revealed something about his identity. Fill in the chart below with what each of these miracles teaches you about Jesus' divine authority.

Passage	What the Miracle Reveals About Jesus
Mark 4:35–41	
Mark 5:1–20	
Mark 5:21–43	
Mark 6:30–44	
Mark 8:22–25	

4. When Jesus healed people, he often linked physical healing with spiritual truth. How does that connection help you understand his mission more fully?

5. Jesus said, "The works I do in my Father's name testify about me" (John 10:25). Jesus was referring to the miracles he did while he was on earth, but what "works" has Jesus done in your life? How do they testify about him?

STUDY 5

The One Who Stands Alone

Jesus stands apart from other religious founders in history. Buddha never claimed to be God. Muhammad insisted he was not divine but merely Allah's prophet. Moses, though chosen and empowered by God, made no claim of divinity and admitted his own human flaws. Jesus broke the mold. He didn't point beyond himself to some distant deity; he pointed *to himself* as God come near. He didn't say, "I'll show you the way" or "I'll show you the truth." He said, "I am the way and the truth and the life" (John 14:6). He didn't offer principles for better living. He offered himself as *life* itself.

Think about this. Every other teacher said, "Follow my words." Jesus said, "Follow me." Every other path points *toward* truth. Jesus claimed to *be* the destination. It's either breathtaking blasphemy or the greatest revelation the world has ever heard. Jesus said that he was *the way* to God: "No one comes to the Father except through me" (John 14:6). Such words were not arrogance but accuracy, for Jesus was God.

Jesus backed up his claims by doing the one thing no one else could: *resurrection*. Buddha's body was cremated and the ashes were placed in monuments. Muhammad's tomb in Medina draws many pilgrims. Confucius lies buried in Qufu, China.[45] But Jesus' tomb in Jerusalem stands empty. Paul put it plainly: "If Christ has not been raised, our preaching is useless and so is your faith" (1 Corinthians 15:14).

Christianity doesn't hinge on a philosophy or moral code but on a historical event. This is why Christianity spread like wildfire even under persecution. The apostles didn't travel the world preaching a lifestyle improvement plan. They proclaimed a risen Savior they had seen with their own eyes. Their courage in the face of torture and death makes no sense apart from one reality: They truly believed they had encountered the living Christ.

Jesus isn't one option among many spiritual guides. He is categorically different—the only one who claimed to be God, provided evidence for it, and confirmed it through his resurrection. As Peter declared, "Salvation is found in no one else, for there is no other name under heaven given to mankind by which we must be saved" (Acts 4:12).

Readings: John 14:1-7; Acts 4:6-12; 1 Timothy 2:1-7

1. Read John 14:1–7. When Jesus told the disciples that he was going to his "Father's house" and they "[knew] the way" (verses 2, 4), the disciple Thomas was confused. "Lord," he said, "we don't know where you are going, so how can we know the way?" (verse 5). So what did Jesus reveal about the way to God?

2. When you consider Jesus' claim that he is the *only* way to God, how is it different from the way other spiritual leaders in history have described the path to God?

3. Read Acts 4:6–12. How did Peter respond when the Jewish leaders asked "by what power or what name" (verse 7) the lame man had been healed? What did Peter boldly proclaim—in spite of persecution—was the only way to salvation?

4. Read 1 Timothy 2:1–7. What does Paul mean when he says that Jesus is the "one mediator between God and mankind" (verse 5)?

5. George Lucas said in an interview, "When I was ten years old, I asked my mother, 'If there's only one God, why are there so many religions?' I've been pondering that question ever since, and the conclusion I've come to is that all religions are true."[46] This form of religious pluralism is the belief that all paths ultimately lead to God. Why do think this kind of thinking is so commonplace in the world today?

Based on what you've studied this week, what is the error in this way of thinking?

How would you respond—graciously but clearly—to someone who said this to you?

Catch Up & Read Ahead

Connect with a fellow group member this week and discuss some of the key insights from this session. Use any of the following prompts to help guide your discussion.

- What stood out to you from C. S. Lewis's statement that Jesus must either be a liar, lunatic, or Lord—and there is no other option available?
- How does Jesus' fulfillment of specific and detailed Old Testament prophecies strengthen your confidence in his identity as the Son of God?
- Why is it important that Jesus didn't just *point* people to truth but actually claimed to *be* the truth and the only way to God?
- What do you personally believe makes Jesus and Christianity unique from all the other religions that are in the world?
- How could you share this week's evidence for Jesus' divinity with someone who views him as only a good teacher?

Use this time to go back and complete any of the study and reflection questions from previous days that you weren't able to finish. Make a note below of any revelations you've had and reflect on any growth or personal insights you've gained.

Read chapter 9 in *Demolishing Doubt* before the next group gathering. Use the space below to note anything that stands out to you or encourages you.

WEEK 4 *at a Glance*

THIS WEEK'S READING	Chapter 9 in *Demolishing Doubt*
GROUP MEETING	Read the Welcome and Connect with the group (page 92) Watch the video and take notes (pages 93–94) Discuss the questions that follow (page 95) Respond to the teaching and Pray (page 96)
PERSONAL STUDIES:	
STUDY 1	"The Fact That Changed History" (pages 99–102)
STUDY 2	"Eyewitnesses to the Resurrection" (pages 103–106)
STUDY 3	"The Testimony of a Transformed Life" (pages 107–110)
STUDY 4	"The Only Explanation" (pages 111–114)
STUDY 5	"The Foundation of Faith" (pages 115–118)
CATCH UP & READ AHEAD (BEFORE WEEK 5 GROUP MEETING)	Connect with someone in your group Complete any unfinished studies (page 119)
NEXT WEEK'S READING	Chapter 10 and conclusion in *Demolishing Doubt*

SESSION FOUR

DID JESUS REALLY RISE FROM THE DEAD?

"He is not here; he has risen! Remember how he told you, while he was still with you in Galilee: 'The Son of Man must be delivered over to the hands of sinners, be crucified and on the third day be raised again.'"

LUKE 24:6-7

WELCOME | READ ON YOUR OWN

Lee Strobel, a former journalist for the *Chicago Tribune*, wrote that even as an atheist, he understood that Christianity rises or falls on the resurrection of Jesus. "Easter is the ball-game," he said. "I had seen lots of corpses during my career as a reporter, but none of them ever regained life, especially after three days. Dead bodies stay dead."[47]

Such a scenario—of a dead body coming back to life—is inconceivable given our understanding of the natural world. Yet this is precisely what Christians claim happened with Jesus. He was executed by crucifixion—a death the Romans had perfected to be both excruciating and certain. His death was verified by professional executioners. He was buried in a tomb. And then, three days later, he was very much alive.

Christianity stands on this single event. The resurrection is not a side note to the Christian faith; it is the cornerstone. It confirms Jesus' divine identity, displays God's power over death, secures our forgiveness, and guarantees our future resurrection. Remove Jesus' resurrection, and Christianity collapses into mere wishful thinking.

The early believers didn't ask anyone to accept this blindly. They pointed to evidence: an empty tomb no one could explain away, hundreds of eyewitnesses who saw Jesus alive, transformed disciples, and a church that exploded across the Roman world despite violent persecution. They invited investigation—just as Jesus himself had.

In this session, you will embark on that same investigation. The resurrection is not a comforting legend or a spiritual metaphor; it is a historical event supported by compelling evidence. The tomb was empty. Jesus did appear to those who knew him best. And because of that, the world—and our place in it—can never be the same.

CONNECT | 10 MINUTES

Take a few minutes to share anything that spoke to you in last week's personal study. Then discuss this question:

> Why do you think the resurrection is so central to Christianity?

WATCH | 25 MINUTES

Watch the video for this session. Below is an outline of the key points covered during the teaching. Record any key concepts that stand out to you.

OUTLINE

I. The resurrection is the cornerstone and anchor of the Christian faith.

A. Christianity is historically "falsifiable"—if you can somehow prove the resurrection didn't occur, then you can completely upend the Christian faith.

B. Those who witnessed the resurrection in the first century had more hoops to jump through than we do in our modern scientific time period.

C. The Gospel writers would not likely have said that women were the first witnesses to Jesus' resurrection if they were inventing the story.

D. Christianity is a living relationship with Jesus—not a musty religion—and the resurrection confirms Jesus' trustworthiness and promise of eternal life.

II. Alternative theories of Jesus' resurrection utterly fail under scrutiny.

A. Scholars like Gary Habermas have dismantled competing "naturalistic" theories.

B. Roman execution methods confirm that Jesus actually died on the cross.

C. Medical details in the Gospels align with modern understandings of death.

D. The disciples' own doubts strengthen the case that the resurrection happened.

III. Eyewitness accounts provide compelling evidence for the resurrection.

A. Paul refers to five hundred people who saw the risen Jesus (see 1 Corinthians 15:6).

B. The New Testament invites *verification* and encourages *investigation* of the events.

C. The New Testament authors stress the public nature of Jesus' resurrection.

D. Faith is based on reliable evidence—and the evidence points to an empty tomb.

IV. The resurrection provides hope, purpose, and the promise of eternal life.

A. The resurrection validates Jesus' sacrifice for our sins on the cross.

B. It affirms God's promise to us of a physical and imperishable resurrection body.

C. It provides hope that we will one day be reunited with loved ones.

D. Belief in the resurrection inspires perseverance, courage, and confidence in life.

NOTES

DISCUSS | 35 MINUTES

Discuss what you just watched by answering the following questions.

1. Invite someone to read Matthew 28:1–10. In the first century, women were barred by Jewish law from serving as witnesses in courtroom trials and at religious rituals.[48] However, each of the four Gospels records that women were the first witnesses of Jesus' resurrection (see also Mark 16:1–8; Luke 24:1–10; John 20:1–18). How does this support the claim that the Gospel writers did not just make up the story?

2. Ask someone to continue reading to Matthew 28:11–15. Why do you think the opponents of Jesus (the chief priests) didn't just deny that Jesus' tomb was empty? How does this "enemy attestation" support the claim that Jesus actually rose from the dead?

3. When Jesus was arrested, all the disciples "deserted him and fled" (Mark 14:50). However, some fifty days later, "Peter stood up with the Eleven" and boldly delivered a sermon about Jesus being "Lord and Messiah" (Acts 2:14, 36). How does the disciples' transformation provide evidence that Jesus actually rose from the dead? What transformations have you seen faith produce in people today?

4. Invite someone to read 1 Corinthians 15:12–19. Some of the Corinthian believers were claiming there was no resurrection of the dead. How does Paul use Jesus' own resurrection to counter that claim? Based on Paul's words in this passage, why is the resurrection so important and central to the Christian faith?

5. The early Christians appealed to evidence, not emotion. They pointed to eyewitnesses, historical details, and fulfilled promises. How does that reality strengthen your faith today? How can their example guide you when you share your own faith?

RESPOND | 10 MINUTES

You've examined some of the evidence for Jesus' resurrection—the empty tomb, eyewitness testimony, and transformed disciples. Take a few moments to reflect on what the resurrection means for you personally and how you will share this hope with others.

> "Where, O death, is your victory? Where, O death, is your sting?" The sting of death is sin, and the power of sin is the law. But thanks be to God! He gives us the victory through our Lord Jesus Christ. Therefore, my dear brothers and sisters, stand firm. Let nothing move you. Always give yourselves fully to the work of the Lord, because you know that your labor in the Lord is not in vain.
>
> **1 CORINTHIANS 15:55-58**

Reread this passage and circle anything that stands out to you. Why are those words and phrases especially meaningful? Why are they needed in your life right now?

Paul celebrates the fact that Jesus won the victory over death. How are you living in that victory? How is it shaping your view of death and eternity?

PRAY | 10 MINUTES

Close your time in prayer. Thank Jesus for securing the victory over death. Ask him to help you live in light of that reality and to share the hope you have of an eternity with Christ with others. Pray that God would open the eyes of those who doubt the resurrection so they will see the compelling evidence and experience the transforming power of the risen Christ.

SESSION FOUR

PERSONAL STUDY

In the group time, you explored the cornerstone of the Christian faith—the empty tomb. In this week's personal study, you will dive into the historical evidence for the resurrection, address common objections, and grasp the implications the resurrection has for you. If you are doing this study with a group, continue writing down your responses, as you will be given a few minutes to share your insights at the next session. If you are reading *Demolishing Doubt* alongside this study, you may want to first review chapter 9 of the book.

STUDY 1

The Fact That Changed History

The tomb was empty. Not metaphorically. Not spiritually. It was physically empty. This wasn't a rumor whispered in back alleys. Jesus was buried in a known location. Roman soldiers guarded it. A massive stone sealed the entrance. Yet on Sunday morning, that stone was rolled away and the body was gone.

The Jewish leaders admitted as much. They never claimed his body remained inside. Instead, they spread a desperate alternative—that the disciples stole it. This explanation was still circulating decades later (Matthew 28:11–15). Ironically, the story confirmed the very thing it tried to deny. The tomb was empty and no one could produce the body.

Then there's the testimony of the women. In the first century, a woman's word carried little legal weight. Yet every gospel writer records women as the first to discover the empty tomb. If the story were made up, no one in that culture would invent female witnesses. The only reason to include them is simple. It happened that way.

The geography also matters. The Christian movement didn't begin in some faraway place. It exploded in Jerusalem, the very city where Jesus was crucified and buried. The apostles publicly declared his resurrection just a short walk from the tomb. If the body had still been there, the religious leaders could have ended the whole thing by opening the tomb and displaying the corpse. But they couldn't because the tomb was empty.

Some claim the women went to the wrong tomb in their grief. But the Gospels state that "Mary Magdalene and Mary the mother of Joseph saw where [Jesus] was laid" (Mark 15:47), and the disciples would have corrected any mistake. If it had been the wrong tomb, authorities could have also checked the right one and found the body.

Others suggest that Jesus merely fainted and later revived. However, Roman soldiers were tasked with ensuring crucified victims were dead. In Jesus' case, a soldier "pierced Jesus' side with a spear" (John 19:34), producing a flow of blood and water—clear signs of fatal trauma. Even if Jesus had somehow staggered out of the grave half alive, his battered condition would have hardly inspired his followers to proclaim him Lord of life.

The empty tomb demands an answer. Every human explanation collapses under scrutiny. The simplest and most consistent explanation remains the one the early Christians boldly proclaimed: God raised Jesus from the dead.

Readings: Matthew 28:1–10; Mark 16:1–8; Luke 24:1–12; John 20:1–9

1. Read each of the four Gospel accounts about the empty tomb. Skeptics often cite differences in these accounts as evidence the Gospel writers made up the story of the resurrection and couldn't get their details straight. However, how would it actually point to *collusion* between the writers if every firsthand account was identical?

2. Review Matthew 28:1–10. What details does Matthew include that are not in the other Gospels? What details does Matthew cite that are different from the others?

3. Review Luke 24:1–12. What details does Luke include that are not in the other Gospels? What details does Luke cite that are different from the others?

4. Review John 20:1–19. Who is the eyewitness that John focuses on? What details does he include about his and Peter's reaction to the news that Jesus' tomb was empty?

5. Now consider what all the Gospel accounts have in common. In the table below, list the key point on which Matthew, Mark, Luke, and John all agree.

Account	Passage	Key Point the Writer Is Making
Matthew	28:5–7	
Mark	16:5–7	
Luke	24:2–7	
John	20:1–2, 6–8	

Based on these accounts, what for certain happened when it came to Jesus' tomb?

STUDY 2

Eyewitnesses to the Resurrection

Hallucinations are private experiences. If you see a pink elephant, you can be sure only you see it. Even if two people do hallucinate at the same time, they don't see the same thing in the same way. This is what makes the resurrection accounts so extraordinary. The Gospels describe multiple occasions where groups of people encountered the risen Jesus together.

Paul gives the most detailed record in 1 Corinthians 15:3–8. Writing around AD 55—barely twenty years after the crucifixion—he lists Jesus' appearances: first to Peter, then to the other disciples, then to more than five hundred believers at once, then to James (his half brother), and then to all the apostles. Paul even adds, "Most of whom are still living" (verse 6). In other words: *If you don't believe me, go ask them yourself.*

Over a span of forty days, Jesus repeatedly appeared—physically. He let Thomas touch his scars, ate meals with his followers, and commissioned them for their mission. The witnesses were diverse. Jesus appeared to individuals and crowds, men and women, devoted followers and hardened skeptics. Such tangible and varied encounters make hallucinations an impossible explanation for the resurrection.

Then there were the skeptics turned believers. James didn't believe Jesus was the Messiah until after the empty tomb (John 7:5). What changed his mind? He encountered Jesus risen from the dead. Paul, for his part, was Christianity's most determined enemy. He hunted down believers until he encountered the risen Christ on the Damascus road.

It's worth remembering that none of the disciples expected a resurrection. When the women reported the empty tomb, the disciples dismissed it as nonsense. These were not gullible men chasing a comforting myth. They were reluctant eyewitnesses who were only convinced because the evidence overwhelmed their doubts.

In total, more than five hundred people saw Jesus alive after his death. They didn't gain power or wealth because of that claim—only persecution. Jesus' resurrection wasn't a legend that evolved over centuries. It was eyewitness testimony from the very beginning of the Christian movement. The voices of these witnesses still echo through history—voices of fishermen and skeptics, brothers and enemies, all united by what they saw.

Readings: 1 Corinthians 15:3–8; [Clement and Polycarp]; Acts 22:1–9

1. Read 1 Corinthians 15:3–8. Paul's use of the phrases "I received" and "passed on to you" (verse 3) indicate that he is stating established tradition. Research has shown that legends take generations to develop, and yet Paul was passing on this established creed only twenty years after Jesus' crucifixion. How does this support the claim that the resurrection happened? How does this reassure you in your beliefs?

> Let us consider, beloved, how the Lord continually proves to us that there shall be a future resurrection, of which He has rendered the Lord Jesus Christ the firstfruits by raising Him from the dead. Let us contemplate, beloved, the resurrection which is at all times taking place. Day and night declare to us a resurrection.
>
> **CLEMENT, *FIRST EPISTLE TO THE CORINTHIANS***

2. Clement, writing around AD 96, was an early church leader who had heard the teachings of the apostles firsthand. (It is likely he had personal contact with Peter.) What does Clement say about the resurrection of Jesus?

> But may the God and Father of our Lord Jesus Christ, and Jesus Christ Himself, who is the Son of God, and our everlasting High Priest, build you up in faith and truth, and in all meekness, gentleness, patience, long-suffering, forbearance, and purity; and may He bestow on you a lot and portion among His saints, and on us with you, and on all that are under heaven, who shall believe in our Lord Jesus Christ, and in His Father, who raised Him from the dead.
>
> **POLYCARP, *EPISTLE TO THE PHILIPPIANS***

3. Polycarp, writing around AD 115, was likely a disciple of the apostle John. What does Polycarp say about Jesus' resurrection? How do these two extrabiblical sources give you confidence that the early church firmly believed in the resurrection?

4. Read Acts 22:1–9. What was Paul's personal testimony of seeing the risen Jesus? How did the experience completely change his view of Christianity?

5. The disciple Thomas, as we have previously discussed, went from doubt in Jesus' resurrection to declaration: "My Lord and my God!" (John 20:28). When was that moment for you? What helped you move from hesitation to conviction?

MY JOURNEY FROM DOUBT TO FAITH		
My hesitation →	**What helped** →	**My conviction**

STUDY 3

The Testimony of a Transformed Life

The night Jesus was arrested, the world of his followers collapsed. Every dream they had built around him—every hope of God's kingdom—seemed to shatter. The sound of the hammer on the nails didn't just pierce the air but also crushed their faith.

When Jesus was arrested, fear replaced faith. Peter swore three times that he didn't even know Jesus (Mark 14:66–72). On Sunday morning, when the women brought news of the empty tomb, the disciples dismissed it as nonsense. When Jesus did appear to them, their first reaction wasn't joy but terror. They thought they were seeing a ghost (Luke 24:37). These were not gullible men; they were crushed, confused, and skeptical.

But then something changed. Within weeks, these same men were standing in the streets of Jerusalem, fearlessly proclaiming, "God has raised this Jesus to life, and we are all witnesses of it" (Acts 2:32). Peter, who had once cowered before a servant girl, now faced the powerful Sanhedrin without flinching. What could explain such transformation?

The disciples didn't merely claim to believe that Jesus rose from the dead. They staked their lives on it. Jesus had told them, "If they persecuted me, they will persecute you also" (John 15:20). As previously noted, the early evidence suggests that James, Peter, Thomas, and Andrew were martyred. Other church traditions state that all of the disciples, except John, were put to death because of their refusal to deny their beliefs.[49]

Skeptics rightly point out that people die for mistaken beliefs all the time. But there's a crucial difference: Those people die for *what they think is true*. The disciples would have known if their message was a lie. They claimed to have seen, touched, and eaten with the risen Jesus. If that wasn't true, they weren't just mistaken; they were deliberately deceiving others. And people don't willingly die for something they know is false.

The disciples' transformation demands an explanation. They didn't die for a myth. They died because they had seen Jesus alive again. Their changed lives remain one of the most compelling pieces of evidence for the reality of the resurrection. And through their testimony, the ripple continues. The resurrection didn't just change *them*; it changes *us*. The story that began in trembling has become the anthem of courage for every believer.

Readings: Matthew 26:69–75; John 21:15–19; Acts 1:4–8; Galatians 1:11–24

1. Take a look at Peter's betrayal of Jesus as recorded in Matthew 26:69–75. Peter had previously declared to Christ, "Even if I have to die with you, I will never disown you" (verse 35). How would you describe Peter's frame of mind at this point?

2. Read John 21:15–19. What did Jesus do for Peter in this scene after the resurrection? What impact do you think this had on Peter's life?

3. Read Acts 1:4–8. What else empowered the disciples to go from fearful and timid to boldly proclaiming the gospel of Christ?

4. Read Galatians 1:11–24. Paul's conversion from persecutor to apostle is another dramatic transformation in the New Testament. In the boxes below, list the characteristics that Paul notes about himself before and after meeting Jesus.

Before (Saul the Persecutor)	**After** (Paul the Apostle)

5. "Let us hold unswervingly to the hope we profess, for he who promised is faithful" (Hebrews 10:23). The hope of the disciples was contagious—and you are now part of the same story.

How could *your* transformation become a testimony to someone watching your life?

Who in particular might benefit from seeing the hope you have in Christ?

What will you do to share the hope you have in Christ with that person?

STUDY 4

The Only Explanation

For two thousand years, skeptics have tried to explain away the resurrection. If Jesus didn't actually rise from the dead, something else must account for the evidence—the empty tomb, the eyewitnesses, and the explosion of faith that followed. Yet every alternative theory collapses under the weight of the facts. Let's review some of these.

First, the *stolen body theory*. This is the oldest theory of them all. Matthew says the religious leaders bribed the soldiers (likely the temple police) to claim the disciples stole the body (see 28:12–13).[50] But it is difficult to believe the guards, who were tasked with keeping watch, would fall asleep on duty at the same time. Furthermore, disturbing tombs was a serious offense, subject at times to the death penalty.[51] Would the terrified disciples really have mustered up the courage to open Jesus' tomb and run the risk of a capital indictment?

Second, the *hallucination theory*. This theory claims the disciples were so overwhelmed with grief they collectively imagined seeing and hearing Jesus after his death. Aside from the fact that science shows mass hallucinations do not exist, it would still mean the body of Jesus was in the tomb. All the Jewish leaders had to do was parade the decaying body of Jesus through the streets of Jerusalem to suppress the disciples' claim.

Third, the *swoon theory*. This theory takes the approach that Jesus didn't actually die but only fainted and later revived in the tomb. But it defies logic. After a brutal flogging, crucifixion, and a spear to his side, are we to believe Jesus somehow pushed aside a massive stone, evaded guards, and convinced his followers that he had conquered death? A half-dead man crawling from a grave wouldn't inspire worship but medical care.

Fourth, the *pagan myth copy theory*. This theory states the New Testament writers copied pagan myths of resurrected figures like Marduk, Adonis, or Osiris. However, a simple reading of these myths shows them to be *very* different from Jesus' resurrection. God chose to pay the penalty for sin so humans could experience eternal life—something that is unique to Christ. Furthermore, this theory still not does explain the empty tomb.

All these theories—and others—crumble under the weight of the evidence. The tomb was empty. The eyewitnesses saw, heard, and touched Jesus. The Romans did actually execute Jesus. The Gospel writers didn't copy older myths. The only explanation that fits is the one the first believers proclaimed with their dying breath: Jesus Christ had risen.

Readings: Matthew 27:62–66; 27:41–42; 28:11–15; 2 Timothy 1:8–10

1. Read Matthew 27:62–66. The stolen body theory is the only one discussed in the Gospels, so we will examine that one in more detail. What was the Pharisees' concern after the body of Jesus was placed in the tomb? What does the fact that they took this concern to Pilate say about how much they feared Jesus even after his death?

2. Pilate refuses to send his troops but tells the Pharisees they have the authority to use the temple police. Why do you think Matthew includes these specific details about how the Jewish leaders sought to make sure the tomb was secure from thievery?

3. Read Matthew 27:41–42 and 28:11–15. At the cross, the Jewish leaders said they would believe in Jesus as the Messiah if he saved himself. But what did these leaders do instead when they heard the report from the temple guards?

4. The Pharisees' worst fears had come true—the body of Jesus had disappeared in spite of all their precautions. In the end, how does their plan to spread the rumor that the disciples stole the body actually support the claim that Jesus rose from the dead?

5. Read 2 Timothy 1:8–10. The early and consistent testimony of the apostles was that Jesus had conquered death. When you put your faith in Christ, you receive power to lead the holy life to which you are called. So, in what area do you need to start living out that calling? Take a few minutes to pray and then do a personal inventory.

Area	How I Need to Start Leading a Holy Life
Relationships	
Thought patterns	
Habits	
Finances/ resources	
Other:	

STUDY 5

The Foundation of Faith

The resurrection of Jesus isn't a footnote in history. It is the singular event that changes everything. Paul put it bluntly: "If Christ has not been raised, your faith is futile; you are still in your sins" (1 Corinthians 15:17). Why is the empty tomb so important?

First, the resurrection *confirms that Jesus is the divine Son of God.* Remember that Jesus didn't just teach moral truths or offer wise sayings. No, he claimed to be God in the flesh and predicted both his death and resurrection. When he stepped out of the tomb, those claims were validated. The resurrection is heaven's exclamation point on Jesus' identity. He is the Son of God with authority over life and death.

Second, the resurrection *proves that Jesus' sacrifice was accepted by God.* On the cross, Jesus bore the sins of humanity and paid the penalty they deserved. When God raised him from the dead, it was divine confirmation the debt was paid in full. Forgiveness isn't a hopeful wish but a settled reality. As Paul wrote, "He was delivered over to death for our sins and was raised to life for our justification" (Romans 4:25).

Third, the resurrection *guarantees your own future resurrection.* Paul says that Jesus is "the firstfruits of those who have fallen asleep" (1 Corinthians 15:20)—the first of the great harvest still to come. Because Jesus rose, you will rise. Death does not have the final word. You will have a resurrected body in God's renewed creation, when everything that was broken at the fall will be restored and made whole again.

Fourth, the resurrection *gives purpose to your perseverance.* Paul ends his resurrection chapter with this charge: "Therefore, my dear brothers and sisters, stand firm. Let nothing move you. Always give yourselves fully to the work of the Lord, because you know that your labor in the Lord is not in vain" (1 Corinthians 15:58). Because Christ lives, nothing you do for him is wasted. Every act of faithfulness echoes into eternity.

The resurrection isn't optional or symbolic. It is the very foundation of Christian faith. It validates Jesus' claims, secures your salvation, promises your own future resurrection, and fills your present with purpose. Everything has changed because he lives.

Read: Romans 4:18-25; 1 Corinthians 15:20-26, 35-44; 1 Peter 1:3-5

1. Read Romans 4:18–25. Paul links Jesus' resurrection directly to your *justification*—your being made right with God. Why is it not just the death of Jesus but also the resurrection that makes your justification complete? How does knowing you have been accepted by and made right with God affect how you approach him today?

2. Read 1 Corinthians 15:20–26. What does Paul mean when he says that "death came through a man" (verse 21)? What kind of "death" is he referring to here?

3. Paul writes that Jesus is the "firstfruits" of those who have died—that his resurrection is the first installment of a greater harvest to come. What does this agricultural image teach you about what is ahead for you as a follower of Jesus?

4. Read 1 Corinthians 15:35–44. Paul here is responding to a question about the kind of body believers will have at the resurrection. Fill in what he says in verses 42–44:

The body that is sown is ______________, it is raised ______________;
it is sown in __________________________, it is raised in ______________;
it is sown in __________________________, it is raised in ______________;
it is sown a ________________ body, it is raised a ______________ body.

Based on this passage, how would you describe what your future resurrected body will be like? What are you most looking forward to about this body?

5. Read 1 Peter 1:3–5. Your hope is "living" in that it is rooted in the resurrection of Jesus. What does it mean for hope to be living rather than abstract or theoretical?

When has that living hope felt the most real to you?

How does it encourage you to know that your hope is active and living?

Catch Up & Read Ahead

Connect with a fellow group member this week and discuss some of the key insights from this session. Use any of the following prompts to help guide your discussion.

- How does the fact that the Jewish leaders never denied the empty tomb nor displayed Jesus' body give you confidence the resurrection is true?
- How does the fact that Jesus was seen by eyewitnesses in a physical place—the region of Judea—give you confidence in his resurrection?
- Why is it important to consider the radical change in the disciples when considering whether the Gospel accounts of the resurrection are true?
- What are some of the theories you've heard people cite about the empty tomb? How would you now respond to those theories?
- How does Jesus' resurrection—the foundation of the Christian faith—personally give you hope in moments of fear, grief, or loss?

Use this time to go back and complete any of the study and reflection questions from previous days that you weren't able to finish. Make a note below of any revelations you've had and reflect on any growth or personal insights you've gained.

Read chapter 10 and the conclusion in *Demolishing Doubt* before the next group gathering. Use the space below to note anything that stands out or encourages you.

WEEK 5 *at a Glance*

THIS WEEK'S READING	Chapter 10 and conclusion in *Demolishing Doubt*
GROUP MEETING	Read the Welcome and Connect with the group (page 122) Watch the video and take notes (pages 123–124) Discuss the questions that follow (page 125) Respond to the teaching and Pray (page 126)
PERSONAL STUDIES:	
STUDY 1	"A Mind Awake to God" (pages 129–132)
STUDY 2	"Knowledge and Trust" (pages 133–136)
STUDY 3	"The Steady Object of Faith" (pages 137–140)
STUDY 4	"Faith and Reason" (pages 141–144)
STUDY 5	"The Wise Builder" (pages 145–148)
WRAP IT UP	Connect with someone in your group Complete any unfinished studies (page 149) Talk about the next study you want to go through together

SESSION FIVE

WHY IS FAITH SO IMPORTANT?

Without faith it is impossible to please God, because anyone who comes to him must believe that he exists and that he rewards those who earnestly seek him.

HEBREWS 11:6

WELCOME | READ ON YOUR OWN

Mark Twain famously quipped, "Faith is believing what you know ain't so," which describes how many people think about faith.[52] Faith is often made to sound like shutting off your brain and believing in spite of the facts to the contrary. Faith and reason are viewed as enemies—the more evidence you demand, the less faith you supposedly have.

This is *not* the faith you find in Scripture. God never asks you for blind belief or naïve optimism. From beginning to end, he invites honest investigation. He doesn't fear your questions; he welcomes them. Jesus performed miracles to provide evidence of who he was. Paul reasoned with skeptics in synagogues and marketplaces. Peter urged believers to "always be prepared to give an answer" for their hope in Christ (1 Peter 3:15).

Biblical faith isn't belief *in spite* of the evidence but trust *because of* the evidence. You can study every safety report on a parachute and be convinced it will open, but until you jump from the plane, that belief changes nothing. Faith is pulling the rip cord. It's stepping from agreement to action, from *knowing about* to actually *trusting in*.

In this study, you've looked at evidence for God's existence, the reliability of the Gospels, the identity of Jesus, and the reality of his resurrection. Each piece of evidence has built a foundation that is not a blind leap into the dark but a confident step into the light. In this final session, you will examine why faith matters and how to hold on to it when doubt knocks at your door. You will see that faith and reason were never meant to be adversaries but allies. Faith isn't *closing* your eyes to reality but *opening* them to a greater one.

CONNECT | 10 MINUTES

Take a few minutes to share anything that spoke to you in last week's personal study. Then discuss this question:

> Why is your faith important to you?

WATCH | 25 MINUTES

Watch the video for this session. Below is an outline of the key points covered during the teaching. Record any key concepts that stand out to you.

OUTLINE

I. Biblical faith is a reasoned trust in God that is grounded in evidence.

A. Biblical faith is not intellectual naïveté or believing what we know to be false.

B. True faith combines evidence of reliability with a personal commitment.

C. "Now faith is confidence in what we hope for and assurance about what we do not see" (Hebrews 11:1).

D. Faith involves thinking critically and grappling with spiritual realities—and leads to peace when we pursue the things of God.

II. Faith is trusting in God's character even in the midst of doubt.

A. Faith depends on the object of trust—Jesus Christ—not the intensity of belief.

B. Doubt is natural and can lead to deeper trust when handled constructively.

C. Trusting God reflects our confidence in his good and reliable character.

D. Faith shapes our priorities and influences how we live and love.

III. Biblical faith trusts in God through the suffering and unanswered prayers.

A. Faith trusts God's fairness and promises, even when life feels unfair or painful.

B. God's presence, not answers, provides comfort and hope in seasons of suffering.

C. The purpose of prayer is to build our intimacy with God—it is not a formula for getting what we want.

D. Maturing in faith involves trusting in God even when we don't fully understand everything that he is doing in our lives.

IV. Trust in God comes through reflecting on his past good works.

A. Reflecting on God's past faithfulness builds future trust.

B. Emotional health and spiritual health are deeply connected.

C. The psalms of David highlight praising God even in the midst of struggles.

D. Gratitude and praise deepen our trust in God and change our perspective on life.

NOTES

DISCUSS | 35 MINUTES

Discuss what you just watched by answering the following questions.

1. Invite someone to read Hebrews 11:1–3. You read this passage at the beginning of this study, but what now especially strikes you about this definition of faith? How does this definition challenge the idea that faith is just a leap into the dark?

2. When you step onto an airplane, you have evidence (based on numerous industry reports) that flying is safe and the plane will hold together. Yet that understanding will do you no good until you actually board the aircraft. How does that illustration apply to faith? Why must faith be evidence *plus* trust for it to be genuine?

3. Ask someone to read Galatians 5:16–26. What does Paul say will happen to those who are being led by the Holy Spirit? What kind of transformation happens in a person who has faith in Jesus—and what type of "fruit" does that person produce?

4. Now invite someone to read James 2:14–17. James warns that faith without works is dead. Why do you think that is true? How do actions give evidence of real faith? In what ways would you say obedience is an act of faith and trust, not duty?

5. Peter wrote, "We did not follow cleverly devised stories when we told you about the coming of our Lord Jesus Christ in power, but we were eyewitnesses of his majesty" (2 Peter 1:16). Why do you think Peter stressed that he was an eyewitness to Jesus' majesty? How would that have helped his readers to have faith in Christ?

RESPOND | 10 MINUTES

You've spent this study thinking deeply about faith—but faith was never meant to stay in your head. It's meant to be lived. Take a few quiet moments to ask God how he might be calling you to put what you've learned into action and take your next step of faith.

> Now the one who has fashioned us for this very purpose is God, who has given us the Spirit as a deposit, guaranteeing what is to come. Therefore we are always confident and know that as long as we are at home in the body we are away from the Lord. For we live by faith, not by sight.
>
> **2 CORINTHIANS 5:5–7**

Faith often looks like obedience before understanding. Why is that so difficult? What helps you obey even when you don't understand the rationale behind God's instruction?

Our culture celebrates certainty and control. How does biblical faith call you to live differently? If faith is trusting God enough to act, what step of obedience or surrender could you take this week to exercise that trust?

PRAY | 10 MINUTES

Close your time in prayer. Thank the Lord for providing evidence for faith and inviting investigation rather than demanding blind belief. Ask him to strengthen your faith and help you trust in him more fully. Pray for opportunities in the weeks and months ahead to continue to share the evidence that you have examined with others who are seeking truth.

SESSION FIVE

PERSONAL STUDY

In this week's final group time, you explored what it means to exercise biblical faith and how to maintain it when doubts arise. This week's personal study will help you understand the relationship between faith and reason, show you what faith looks like when lived out, and equip you to trust God more fully. As you work through each of these exercises, be sure to write down your responses to the questions. If you are reading *Demolishing Doubt* alongside this study, first review chapter 10 and the conclusion of the book.

STUDY 1

A Mind Awake to God

In the culture of today, faith is often caricatured as believing without evidence—or, worse, believing *against* evidence. Skeptics roll their eyes and accuse Christians of blind belief, as if faith were the opposite of reason. But that's not biblical faith at all.

Throughout Scripture, God consistently provides evidence and welcomes honest inquiry. When Moses questioned God's call, the Lord didn't scold him but gave him signs to perform (Exodus 4:1-9). When Gideon wrestled with doubt, God graciously confirmed his promise through the fleece (Judges 6:36-40). When John the Baptist sent messengers to ask if Jesus was truly the Messiah, he wasn't shamed for asking. Jesus just pointed to the proof: *the blind see, the lame walk, lepers are cleansed, the deaf hear* (Matthew 11:2-6).

Jesus regularly appealed to evidence. When Jewish leaders one time accused him of blasphemy, he replied, "Do not believe me unless I do the works of my Father. But if I do them, even though you do not believe me, believe the works, that you may know and understand that the Father is in me, and I in the Father" (John 10:37-38). In other words, Jesus invited them to look at the evidence and draw a reasonable conclusion. Even the resurrection, as we have seen, is presented as a matter of evidence.

This is why *apologetics*—the practice of defending the Christian faith through reasoned arguments and evidence—is deeply biblical. Luke writes that it was Paul's "custom" to reason with people in the synagogues and public squares (Acts 17:2). Peter urged followers of Jesus to "always be prepared to give an answer" for the hope they possessed (1 Peter 3:15). Faith and reason aren't *rivals* but *partners.*

Biblical faith means trusting because of evidence, not in spite of it. You weigh the claims of Jesus—his life, his teachings, his death, his resurrection—and find them compelling. Then you take the next step: personal trust.

Faith doesn't demand absolute proof or perfect certainty. It's not a mathematical equation. But it is reasonable. God has given you good reasons to believe. Real faith isn't a blind leap into the dark—it's a confident step into the light of truth.

Readings: John 10:37-38; 14:11-14; Acts 17:1-4, 16-21

1. Read John 10:37–38. Jesus spoke these words to a group of Jewish opponents who had just picked up stones to put him to death for blasphemy. What evidence does Jesus give them as to whether or not they should believe he is the Son of God?

2. Read John 14:11–14. What evidence does Jesus give to the disciples as to whether or not they should believe that he is "in the Father" (verse 11)? How is this statement to Thomas similar to the one Jesus made to his Jewish opponents?

3. Read Acts 17:1–4. How do you think Paul used "the Scriptures" (the Old Testament) to reason with the Thessalonians and prove that Jesus was the Messiah? What does this teach you about how to share the gospel with those who don't share your faith?

4. Read Acts 17:16–21. The Athenians called Paul a "babbler" (verse 18) when he tried to reason with them. However, what invitation did they extend to Paul? What does this say about how people will react when exposed to the gospel?

5. Jesus' and Paul's approaches show that faith is thoughtful and not naïve. Who has God put in your life who might be ready to have a faith conversation with you? How could you start that conversation? What might be the best way to talk to them?

Person's name: ______________________________

How you might start a conversation on faith:

____

____

____

Best approach to take:

____

____

____

Next step to take:

____

____

____

STUDY 2

Knowledge and Trust

You can believe every right thing about Jesus and still be lost. This is the unsettling warning from James: "You believe that there is one God. Good! Even the demons believe that—and shudder" (James 2:19). Demons have good theology. They know exactly who Jesus is. But their knowledge doesn't save them because they refuse to *submit* to him.

Biblical faith involves both knowledge *and* trust. You need to know who Jesus is—that he is the Son of God, died for your sins, and rose from the dead. But knowing these facts is not enough. Faith isn't just agreeing with a statement; it's entrusting yourself to a Savior. It's surrendering your will, following his lead, and staking your life on his promises.

Think back to the illustration of the plane from this week's group time. You can study everything about it—the engineering, the pilot's credentials, the safety record—and believe completely that it can fly. But until you actually step on board, that knowledge changes nothing. Faith begins the moment you move from *belief in theory* to *trust in action.*

Jesus didn't invite fans but called followers. He said, "Whoever wants to be my disciple must deny themselves and take up their cross and follow me" (Mark 8:34). He wasn't after intellectual agreement but wholehearted allegiance. True faith means obeying Jesus even when it's costly, inconvenient, or unpopular.

Too many people settle for what could be called "cultural Christianity." They grew up in church, know the Bible stories, and can recite Christian doctrine. They *believe* in Jesus, but they have never *trusted* him. They have never surrendered control nor taken that decisive step of moving from knowing *about* Jesus to *walking with* him.

Real faith changes everything. When you truly trust Jesus, it shows. Your obedience becomes an expression of love, not obligation. Your values shift to match his. You find your identity in him instead of chasing approval from others. You are willing to lose comfort or reputation for his sake. James said "faith without deeds is dead" (2:26), not because works earn salvation but because genuine faith always produces transformation.

So, here's the real question: Do you simply believe in Jesus, or have you boarded the plane? Have you staked your life on him? There is a difference between knowing *about* Jesus and truly *knowing* him—the difference between empty belief and saving faith.

Readings: James 2:14–19; Matthew 7:21–23; John 3:16–21

1. Read James 2:14–19. James says that even the demons believe there is one God—that faith must be also accompanied by good works. What are some characteristics of a person who "only believes" versus someone who has a "living faith"?

Belief Alone	Living Faith

2. Read Matthew 7:21–23. Jesus warns that calling him "Lord" without obedience is hollow faith. How do his words sharpen your understanding of being his disciple?

3. Read John 3:16–21. God's promises of eternal life apply to anyone who "believes in [Christ]" (verse 16). When you consider James 2:14–19 and Matthew 7:21–23, what kind of belief is being described here? How might it be different from just intellectual agreement? How might trust or surrender be part of it?

4. *Genuine faith always produces transformation.* Do you agree with this statement? If so, what transformation have you seen in your life as a result of your faith?

5. Jesus said, "Let your light shine before others, that they may see your good deeds and glorify your Father in heaven" (Matthew 5:16). Are people in your life seeing the light of Christ through your actions? If not, what changes could you make this week?

STUDY 3

The Steady Object of Faith

Picture two people standing at the edge of a frozen pond. One feels confident. The ice looks solid, so she steps out. But the other hesitates, anxious and unsure, heart pounding with fear. Yet whether the ice holds them up has nothing to do with how confident they feel. If the ice is solid, it will support them—no matter how weak or strong their faith may be.

The same is true of your faith. The strength of your faith matters less than the reliability of its object. You can have shaky, hesitant, uncertain faith in a strong Savior and still be saved. Or you can have unshakable confidence in the wrong thing and be lost. What matters most isn't how intensely you believe but in whom you're trusting.

Many Christians wrestle with doubt and wonder if their faith is "enough." They compare themselves to others who seem more certain, more emotional, more passionate. They worry that their questions or hesitations somehow disqualify them. But that's not how salvation works. We're not saved by the strength of our faith. We're saved by the strength of our Savior. Even a trembling faith in Jesus saves because he is completely trustworthy.

Doubt doesn't disprove your faith; it deepens it. In fact, the Bible is full of faithful people who wrestled with uncertainty. Thomas doubted until he saw the risen Christ (John 20:25). John the Baptist sent his disciples to ask if Jesus was really the Messiah (Matthew 11:2–3). David poured out his doubts in psalm after psalm. But notice what they all did: They brought their doubts to God. They examined the evidence. They remembered his faithfulness. Thomas's doubt turned to worship when Jesus appeared (John 20:28). John's was met with proof—the blind saw, the lame walked (Matthew 11:4–5). David's despair lifted when he recalled God's past deliverance.

When doubt creeps in, don't deny it and don't drown in guilt. Instead, bring it honestly to God. Revisit what he has done. Remind yourself who he is. Let your faith rest not on the changing temperature of your emotions but on the unchanging character of Christ. Feelings will fluctuate. Certainty will come and go. But Jesus remains the same yesterday, today, and forever (Hebrews 13:8). The question isn't how strong your faith is but how strong your Savior is. And he is strong enough to hold you.

Readings: Matthew 8:23–27; Mark 9:14–24; 1 Corinthians 10:3–4; Hebrews 13:5–8

1. Read Matthew 8:23–27. The disciples panic even though Jesus is right there with them. What does this say about the strength of their faith?

2. How did Jesus respond to the disciples' lack of faith in him? What does the outcome of this story reveal about why you can make Jesus the object of your faith?

3. Read Mark 9:14–24. What led to the demon-possessed boy being brought to Christ? How did he respond when he learned the disciples could not cast out the demon?

4. The boy's father cries out, "I do believe; help me overcome my unbelief!" (verse 24). How does this cry model honest faith? When have you prayed something similar?

5. Read 1 Corinthians 10:3–4 and Hebrews 13:5–8. Jesus never changes, which means his promise to be with you always will stand forever. In the space below, write out three truths about Jesus, "the Rock," that can steady you when your faith feels rocky.

Jesus is . . .

1. ______________________________

2. ______________________________

3. ______________________________

STUDY 4

Faith and Reason

Francis Collins, a renowned physician-scientist and geneticist, once said that "reason and faith go hand in hand—though faith has the added component of revelation."[53] Science (reason) explains the *how* of creation while faith (revelation) addresses the *why*. It is false to believe the two are opposites. Remember, Jesus said, "Love the Lord your God with all your heart and with all your soul and with all your *mind*" (Matthew 22:37, emphasis added).

Some of the greatest thinkers in the history of the world have been followers of Christ. Augustine built a framework of philosophy and theology that still shapes culture today. Thomas Aquinas integrated faith and logic so deeply that both the church and universities continue to quote him. Blaise Pascal was a mathematical genius and passionate believer. Isaac Newton revolutionized science while writing more about the Bible than physics. Francis Collins, for his part, calls science "an opportunity for worship."[54] None of these individuals saw faith and reason as enemies but as partners in pursuing truth.

Reason is the tool that God has given you to examine evidence, weigh ideas, and draw conclusions. But reason alone has boundaries. Again, it can explain *how* things work but not always *why*. It can measure the universe but not its meaning. This is where faith steps in—not to replace reason but to carry it farther than logic alone can go.

The truth is that everyone has faith in something. The atheist has faith that the universe appeared from nothing without cause. The evolutionist has faith that consciousness somehow emerged from lifeless matter. The humanist has faith that human capabilities and values will win the day. Every worldview requires trust in unprovable assumptions. The question isn't whether you have faith but in *whom* or *what* you place that faith.

"The heart of the discerning acquires knowledge, for the ears of the wise seek it out" (Proverbs 18:15). Christianity doesn't fear questions; it invites them. It doesn't silence reason; it engages it. It doesn't call people to ignore knowledge; it instructs them to seek it. The gospel is built on evidence, history, and claims that can be investigated. Does that mean we have airtight answers for everything? No. But it means our faith is reasonable.

So don't settle for the false choice between faith and reason. God designed your mind as much as your heart, and he calls you to use both. To love God fully is to think deeply, question honestly, and believe confidently.

Readings: Isaiah 1:18–20; 2 Corinthians 10:1–6; Matthew 17:19–20

1. Read Isaiah 1:18–20. God spoke these words to the people of Judah as an invitation for them to return to him. What "matter" is God laying out to them about their spiritual condition? What does he wish to "settle" with them (verse 18)?

2. What does God's invitation reveal about his character and the kind of relationship he wants to have with you? Is there a specific matter about your spiritual condition that he is inviting you to settle with him? Why might it be helpful for you to do that?

3. Read 2 Corinthians 10:1–6 and notice the "appeal" that Paul makes to believers in Christ. What would it look like for you to "take captive every thought" and "make it obedient to Christ" (verse 5)? How about taking your doubting thoughts captive?

A Doubting Thought I Need to Take Captive

The Truth I Will Replace It With

The Action I Will Take

4. How can disciplined thinking protect your mind from confusion or false ideas? What (or who) could help you practice more disciplined thinking?

5. Read Matthew 17:19–20. Remember that the question isn't whether you have faith but in *whom* or *what* you place your faith. What does Jesus say about the power of faith? Overall, why does it make reasonable sense to put your faith in him?

STUDY 5

The Wise Builder

Five weeks of exploration have brought you here. You've examined evidence for God's existence, the historical reliability of the Gospels, the divine identity of Jesus, the reality of the resurrection, and the true nature of biblical faith. You have seen that Christianity isn't wishful thinking but reasoned faith grounded in truth. Now comes the crucial question: *What will you do with everything that you've discovered?*

Jesus once told a story about two builders. One built his house on rock, while the other built his house on sand. Both faced storms, but only one house stood firm (Matthew 7:24–27). Jesus went on to explain the difference wasn't in the materials but in obedience. The wise builder heard his words and acted on them. The foolish builder heard but never responded. The lesson is clear: Evidence alone doesn't save, and knowledge alone doesn't transform. Faith must move from information to action. You have to build your life on the rock by actually trusting Jesus and following his commands.

The call today is to be a wise builder. You have solid reasons for your hope in Christ—truths that serve as an anchor when storms come and give you confidence to share the message of the gospel. You can answer questions with grace, engage doubt with wisdom, and show that Christian faith isn't blind—it's beautifully reasonable.

But don't stop there! Jesus said, "Ask and it will be given to you; seek and you will find; knock and the door will be opened to you" (Matthew 7:7). In the original Greek, this instruction is more accurately translated, "Keep asking . . . keep seeking . . . keep knocking." The command is for an ongoing effort in seeking wisdom. So keep building. Keep wrestling. Keep asking the hard questions—and allow them to drive you closer to God.

Most importantly, live out what you believe. Let the truth move from your head to your hands. Let the evidence become obedience and the conviction become compassion. Remember that Jesus isn't looking for admirers but followers. He does something much more than just invite you to *believe* in him—he invites you to *belong* to him. He wants to steady your steps when the ground shakes and carry you when your faith feels weak. What he desires most is your heart . . . one fully surrendered and fully alive in his love.

The foundation has been laid. The evidence is solid. Now build your life on the rock. The storms will come, but so will the strength to stand. The best is yet to come.

Readings: Matthew 7:24–27; Romans 10:9–10; 2 Timothy 1:12–13

1. Read Matthew 7:24–27. In this parable, Jesus talks about two kinds of builders: a wise one and a foolish one. Notice that both builders went through the same type of storm. So what distinguished the wise builder from the foolish builder?

Wise Builder	Foolish Builder

2. What does this parable reveal about the importance of not only *hearing* Jesus' words but actually putting them into *practice*? What is the promise that Jesus gives to the person who chooses to obey his words?

3. Read Romans 10:9–10. Paul writes that salvation includes declaring "with your mouth" that Jesus is Lord and believing "in your heart" that God raised him from the dead. Why do you think both heart-belief and public confession matter?

4. Read 2 Timothy 1:12–13. As Paul came to the end of his life, and in spite of all the suffering he had endured, he could say, "I know whom I have believed" (verse 12). As you come to the end of this study, can you say the same? What has Jesus made real to you that enables you to say with Paul, "I know whom I have believed"?

5. Looking back over the past five weeks, what has been the most significant insight or discovery for you? What's most shaped or grown your understanding of faith?

Session	Key Insight That Shaped My Faith
❶ Evidence for God	
❷ Historical reliability of the Gospels	
❸ Evidence that Jesus was the Son of God	
❹ Evidence that the resurrection was real	
❺ What faith is and why it matters to your life	

Wrap It Up

Connect with a fellow group member this week and discuss some of the key insights from this session. Use any of the following prompts to help guide your discussion.

- How has this study changed your understanding of faith? Why is the *object* of your faith more important than the *strength* of your faith?
- How have you seen God meet you in your doubts? How will you use what you've learned in conversations with others who have doubts?
- As you look back over this entire study, which truth most deepened your relationship with Jesus? Why that particular truth?
- What step of obedience do you sense God is inviting you to take as a result of what you have learned? When will you take that step?
- What habits have you developed that will help you to continue to grow?

Use this time to go back and complete any of the study and reflection questions that you weren't able to finish. Make a note below of any revelations you've had and reflect on any growth or personal insights you've gained. Finally, talk with your group about what study you want to go through next. Put a date on the calendar for when you will meet next to study God's Word and dive deeper into community.

LEADER'S GUIDE

Thank you for your willingness to lead your group through this study! What you have chosen to do is valuable and will make a difference in the lives of others. *Demolishing Doubt* is a five-session Bible study built around video content and small-group interaction. As the group leader, imagine yourself as the host of a party. Your job is to take care of your guests by managing the details so that when your guests arrive, they can focus on one another and on the interaction around the topic for that session.

Your role as the group leader is not to answer all the questions or reteach the content—the video and study guide will do most of that work. Your job is to guide the experience and cultivate your small group into a connected and engaged community. This will make it a place for members to process, question, and reflect—not necessarily to receive more instruction. There are several elements in this leader's guide that will help you as you structure your study and reflection time, so be sure to follow along and take advantage of each one.

BEFORE YOU BEGIN

Before your first meeting, make sure the group members have a copy of this study guide. Alternately, you can hand out the study guides at your first meeting and give the members some time to look over the material and ask any preliminary questions. Also, make sure the group members are aware they have access to the streaming videos at any time by following the instructions provided with this guide. During your first meeting, ask them to provide their names, phone numbers, and email addresses so that you can keep in touch.

Generally, the ideal size for a group is eight to ten people, which will ensure that everyone has enough time to participate in discussions. If you have more people, break up the main group into smaller subgroups. Encourage those who show up at the first meeting to commit to attending the duration of the study, as this will help the group members get to know one another, create stability for the group, and help you know how best to prepare to lead the participants through the material.

Each session begins with an opening reflection in the Welcome section. The questions that follow in the Connect section serve as icebreakers to get the group members thinking about the topic. In the rest of the study, it's generally not a good idea to have everyone answer every question—a free-flowing discussion is more desirable. But with the icebreaker question, you can go around the circle and ask each person to respond. Encourage shy people to share, but don't force them.

At your first meeting, let the group members know each session contains a personal study section they can use to continue to engage with the content until the next meeting. While doing this section is optional, it will help cement the concepts presented during the group study time so they can better understand how to demolish doubt in their lives.

Let them know that if they choose to do so, they can watch the video for the next session by accessing the streaming code provided with this study guide. Invite them to bring any questions and insights to your next meeting, especially if they had a breakthrough moment or didn't understand something.

PREPARATION FOR EACH SESSION

As the leader, there are a few things you should do to best prepare for each meeting:

- **Read through the session.** This will help you become more familiar with the content and know how to structure the discussion times.

- **Decide how the videos will be used.** Determine whether you want the members to watch the videos ahead of time (again, via the streaming access code provided with this study guide) or together as a group.

- **Decide which questions you want to discuss.** Based on the length of your group discussions, you may not be able to get through all the questions. So look over the discussion questions provided in each session and mark which ones you definitely want to cover.

- **Be familiar with the questions you want to discuss.** When the group meets, you'll be watching the clock, so make sure you are familiar with the questions you have selected.

- **Pray for your group.** Pray for your group members and ask God to lead them as they study his Word and listen to his Spirit.

In many cases, there will be no one "right" answer to the questions. Answers will vary, especially when the group members are sharing their personal experiences.

STRUCTURING THE DISCUSSION TIME

You will need to determine with your group how long you want your meetings to last so that you can plan your time accordingly. Suggested times for each section have been provided in this study guide, and if you adhere to these times, your group will meet for ninety minutes. However, many groups like to meet for two hours. If this describes your particular group, follow the times listed in the right-hand column of the chart given below.

Section	90 Minutes	120 Minutes
CONNECT (discuss one or more of the opening questions for the session)	10 minutes	20 minutes
WATCH (watch the teaching material together and take notes)	25 minutes	20 minutes
DISCUSS (discuss the study questions you selected ahead of time)	35 minutes	50 minutes
RESPOND (write down any key takeaways)	10 minutes	15 minutes
PRAY (pray together and dismiss)	10 minutes	15 minutes

As the group leader, it is up to you to keep track of the time and to keep things on schedule. You might want to set a timer for each segment so that both you and the group members know when the time is up. (There are some good phone apps for timers that play a gentle chime or other pleasant sound instead of a disruptive noise.)

Don't be concerned if members are quiet or slow to share. People are often quiet when they are pulling together their ideas, and this might be a new experience for some of them. Just ask a question and let it hang in the air until someone shares. You can then say, "Thank you. What about others? What came to you when you watched that portion of the teaching?"

GROUP DYNAMICS

Leading a group through *Demolishing Doubt* will prove to be highly rewarding both to you and your group members. But you still may encounter challenges along the way! Discussions can get off track. Group members may not be sensitive to the needs and ideas of others. Some might worry that they will be expected to talk about matters that make them feel awkward. Others may express comments that result in disagreements.

To help ease this strain on you and the group, consider the following ground rules:

- When someone raises a question or comment that is off the main topic, suggest you deal with it another time, or, if you feel led to go in that direction, let the group know that you will be spending some time discussing it.
- If someone asks a question that you don't know how to answer, admit it and move on. At your discretion, feel free to invite group members to comment on questions that call for personal experience.
- If you find that one or two people are dominating the discussion time, direct a few questions to others in the group. Outside the main group time, ask the more dominating members to help you draw out the quieter ones. Work to make them part of the solution instead of part of the problem.
- When a disagreement occurs, encourage the group members to process the matter in love. Encourage those on opposite sides to restate what they heard the other side say about the matter, and then invite each side to evaluate if that perception is accurate. Lead the group in examining other passages related to the topic and look for common ground.

When any of these issues arise, encourage your group members to follow these words from Scripture: "Love one another" (John 13:34); "If it is possible, as far as it depends on you, live at peace with everyone" (Romans 12:18); "Whatever is true . . . noble . . . right . . . pure . . . lovely . . . admirable . . . if anything is excellent or praiseworthy—think about these things" (Philippians 4:8); and, "Everyone should be quick to listen, slow to speak and slow to become angry" (James 1:19). This will make your group time more rewarding and beneficial for everyone who attends.

Thank you for taking the time to lead your group. You are making a difference in your group members' lives and helping them know that what the Bible says about God and their faith is accurate, reliable, and true.

FOR FURTHER READING

Bishop, Robert C., Larry L. Funck, Raymond J. Lewis, Stephen O. Moshier, and John H. Walton. *Understanding Scientific Theories of Origins: Cosmology, Geology, and Biology in Christian Perspective.* InterVarsity, 2018.

Chatraw, Joshua D., and Mark D. Allen. *Apologetics at the Cross: An Introduction for Christian Witness.* Zondervan Academic, 2018.

Collins, Francis S. *Belief: Readings on the Reason for Faith.* HarperCollins, 2010.

Copan, Paul. *How Do You Know You're Not Wrong? Responding to Objections That Leave Christians Speechless.* Baker, 2005.

Craig, William Lane. *God, Are You There?: Five Reasons God Exists and Three Reasons It Makes a Difference.* Wipf & Stock, 2023.

Davies, Paul. *The Cosmic Blueprint: New Discoveries in Nature's Creative Ability to Order the Universe.* Templeton Press, 2004.

Flew, Antony. *There Is a God: How the World's Most Notorious Atheist Changed His Mind.* HarperOne, 2008.

Geisler, Norman L., and Frank Turek. *I Don't Have Enough Faith to Be an Atheist.* Crossway, 2004.

Green, Michael. *Running from Reality.* InterVarsity, 1983.

Groothuis, Douglas. *Christian Apologetics: A Comprehensive Case for Biblical Faith.* InterVarsity, 2022.

Habermas, Gary R., and Michael R. Licona. *The Case for the Resurrection of Jesus.* Kregel Publications, 2004.

Keller, Timothy. *The Reason for God: Belief in an Age of Skepticism.* Penguin, 2008.

Knechtle, Cliffe. *Give Me an Answer That Satisfies My Heart and My Mind.* InterVarsity, 1986.

Knechtle, Cliffe. *Help Me Believe: Direct Answers to Real Questions.* InterVarsity, 2000.

Lennox, John. *Can Science Explain Everything?* Good Book Company, 2009.

Lewis, C. S. *Mere Christianity.* Macmillan, 1951.

McDowell, Josh, and Sean McDowell. *Evidence for Jesus: Timeless Answers for Tough Questions About Christ.* Thomas Nelson, 2023.

McDowell, Josh, and Sean McDowell. *Evidence That Demands a Verdict: Life-Changing Truth for a Skeptical World.* Thomas Nelson, 2017.

McDowell, Sean, general editor. *Apologetics for an Ever-Changing Culture: A Biblical and Culturally Relevant Approach to Talking About God*. Harvest House, 2025.

McDowell, Sean. *The Fate of the Apostles: Examining the Martyrdom Accounts of the Closest Followers of Jesus*. Routledge, 2018.

McLaughlin, Rebecca. *Confronting Christianity: 12 Hard Questions for the World's Largest Religion*. Crossway, 2019.

McLaughlin, Rebecca. *10 Questions Every Teen Should Ask (and Answer) About Christianity*. Crossway, 2021.

Moreland, J. P. *Scientism and Secularism: Learning to Respond to a Dangerous Ideology*. Crossway, 2018.

Neill, Stephen. *Christian Faith and Other Faiths*. InterVarsity, 1984.

Orr-Ewing, Amy. *Is the Bible Intolerant?* InterVarsity, 2006.

Orr-Ewing, Amy. *Why Trust the Bible? Answers to Ten Tough Questions*. Revised edition. InterVarsity, 2020.

Sire, James W. *Habits of the Mind: Intellectual Life as a Christian Calling*. InterVarsity, 2000.

Stoner, Peter W. *Science Speaks: An Evaluation of Certain Christian Evidences*. Moody Press, 1963.

Stott, John. *Being a Christian*. InterVarsity, 2016.

VanderKam, James and Peter Flint. *Meaning of the Dead Sea Scrolls: Their Significance for Understanding the Bible, Judaism, Jesus, and Christianity*. HarperOne, 2004.

Wallace, J. Warner. *Cold-Case Christianity: A Homicide Detective Investigates the Claims of the Gospels*. Expanded edition. David C. Cook, 2023.

Wright, Christopher J. H. *The God I Don't Understand: Reflections on Tough Questions of Faith*. Zondervan, 2009.

NOTES

1. Stanley L. Miller, "A Production of Amino Acids Under Possible Primitive Earth Conditions," *Science* 117, no. 3046 (1953): 528–529, https://doi.org/10.1126/science.117.3046.528.
2. Augustine, *The Confessions*, book 1, chapter 1.
3. "List of Fine-Tuning Parameters," Discovery Institute, accessed January 9, 2026, https://www.discovery.org/a/fine-tuning-parameters/.
4. Paul Davies, *The Cosmic Blueprint: New Discoveries in Nature's Creative Ability to Order the Universe* (Templeton Press, 2004), chapter 14.
5. Malcolm W. Browne, "Clues to Universe Origin Expected," *New York Times*, March 12, 1978, https://www.nytimes.com/1978/03/12/archives/clues-to-universe-origin-expected-the-making-of-the-universe.html.
6. Lawrence M. Krauss, *A Universe from Nothing: Why There Is Something Rather than Nothing* (Atria Books, 2013).
7. "Hubble Finds Proof That the Universe Is Expanding," *A Science Odyssey*, PBS, accessed January 9, 2026, https://www.pbs.org/wgbh/aso/databank/entries/dp29hu.html.
8. "Penzias and Wilson Discover Cosmic Microwave Radiation," *A Science Odyssey*, PBS, accessed January 9, 2026, https://www.pbs.org/wgbh/aso/databank/entries/dp65co.html.
9. Ernie Tretkoff, "February 1917: Einstein's Biggest Blunder," *APS News*, American Physical Society, July 1, 2005, https://www.aps.org/apsnews/2005/07/february-1917-einsteins-biggest-blunder.
10. Jonathan McLatchie, "A Beginner's Guide to the Kalam Cosmological Argument," Solas, March 23, 2020, https://www.solas-cpc.org/a-beginners-guide-to-the-kalam-cosmological-argument/.
11. Blaise Pascal, *Pensées*, section vii, number 425.
12. C. S. Lewis, *Mere Christianity* (HarperOne, 2001), book 3, chapter 10.
13. Augustine, *Confessions*, translated by Henry Chadwick (Oxford University Press, 1991), book 1, chapter 1.
14. Charles Darwin, *On the Origin of Species: By Means of Natural Selection, or the Preservation of Favored Races in the Struggle for Life* (John Murray, 1859), chapter 6.
15. "ACGT," National Human Genome Research Institute, updated January 9, 2026, https://www.genome.gov/genetics-glossary/acgt.
16. "First Complete Sequence of a Human Genome," National Institutes of Health, April 12, 2022, https://www.nih.gov/news-events/nih-research-matters/first-complete-sequence-human-genome.
17. Antony Flew, *There Is a God: How the World's Most Notorious Atheist Changed His Mind* (HarperOne, 2008).
18. James VanderKam and Peter Flint, *Meaning of the Dead Sea Scrolls: Their Significance for Understanding the Bible, Judaism, Jesus, and Christianity* (HarperOne, 2004).
19. Jeremy D. Lyon, "What the Dead Sea Scrolls Reveal About the Bible's Reliability," Bible Study Magazine, February 8, 2022, https://www.logos.com/grow/bsm-what-the-dead-sea-scrolls-reveal-about-the-bibles-reliability/.
20. Mark L. Strauss, *Four Portraits, One Jesus: A Survey of Jesus and the Gospels*, 2nd ed. (Zondervan Academic, 2020), 58.

21. Clement of Alexandria claimed that Mark wrote while Peter was ministering in Rome. Church tradition states that Peter was martyred during the persecutions of the emperor Nero, around AD 64–67. This would allow for a date of Mark anytime from the mid 50s to the early 60s. See Walter W. Wessel and Mark L. Strauss, *The Expositor's Bible Commentary*, volume 9, "Mark" (Zondervan Academic, 2010), 685.
22. The earliest documents referring to Matthew's Gospel are the epistles of Ignatius (especially *To the Smyrnaeans*), written c. AD 110–115, so the end of the first century is the latest date for Matthew to have been written. See D. A. Carson, *The Expositor's Bible Commentary*, volume 9, "Matthew" (Zondervan Academic, 2010), 43. There is evidence in Luke's Gospel and in Acts (also written by Luke) of a troublesome time begun by the Neronian persecution, which took place c. AD 64–67. This argues for a date of no earlier than AD 70, while historical events absent in Luke and Acts point to a date of writing in the first century. See Walter L. Liefeld and David W. Pao, *The Expositor's Bible Commentary*, volume 10, "Luke" (Zondervan Academic, 2007), 33.
23. There are references in John 9:22, 12:42, and 16:2 of Jewish believers being excommunicated from the synagogues. In AD 85, the rabbis of Palestine instituted such expulsions for Christians (Rabbi Gamaliel II). There is therefore a remarkable consensus of scholarly opinion that the Gospel of John was published sometime between AD 80 and 100. See Gary M. Burge, *The NIV Application Commentary*, "John" (Zondervan Academic, 2000), 28.

24. The earliest surviving biography of Alexander the Great, *Historiae Alexandri Magni*, was written by the Roman historian Quintus Curtius Rufus during the first century AD. Alexander the Great is believed to have lived from 356–323 BC.
25. "The Gallic Bore," Dwane Thomas, accessed January 9, 2026, https://dwanethomas.com/the-gallic-bore/.
26. Daniel Wallace, "The Number of Variants," Biblical Training, accessed January 9, 2026, https://www.biblicaltraining.org/learn/institute/nt605-textual-criticism/nt605-03-the-number-of-variants.
27. Scott Stein, "A Book Like No Other," Prepared to Answer, September 18, 2017, https://preparedtoanswer.org/article/8340-a-book-like-no-other.
28. Will Varner, "What Is the Importance of the Dead Sea Scrolls?" Associates for Biblical Research, May 21, 2008, https://biblearchaeology.org/research/topics/ancient-manuscripts/3590-what-is-the-importance-of-the-dead-sea-scrolls.
29. "Luke: A Historian of the First Rank!" Bible Apologetics—A Daily Devotional, February 3, 2021, https://bibleapologetics.org/luke-a-historian-of-the-first-rank/.
30. "Expositor's Bible Commentary" on Acts 17, Bible Hub, accessed January 9, 2026, https://biblehub.com/commentaries/expositors/acts/17.htm.
31. Bryan Windle, "Top Ten Discoveries Related to Jesus," Bible Archaeology Report, April 2, 2021, https://biblearchaeologyreport.com/2021/04/02/top-ten-discoveries-related-to-jesus/.
32. Archaeological evidence, primarily the fragmentary Lapis Tiburtinus inscription (Tivoli inscription) and Roman coins, suggests Quirinius served in Syria *twice*, possibly as a special legate for a census (c. 6–4 BC) and later as governor (AD 6), reconciling Luke's Gospel with Josephus's account of a later census, though the inscription's owner and specific role remain debated by scholars.
33. Flavius Josephus, *The Antiquities of the Jews*, translated by William Whiston (Wilder Publications, 2009), book 18, chapter 3, section 3.
34. Josephus, *The Antiquities of the Jews*, book 20, chapter 9, section 1.
35. Tacitus, *Annals, translated by Cynthia Damon* (Penguin Publishing Group, 2013), book 15, chapter 44.
36. Pliny the Younger, *The Letters of the Younger Pliny* (Penguin Classics, 1963), book 10, letter 96.
37. Sean McDowell, *The Fate of the Apostles: Examining the Martyrdom Accounts of the Closest Followers of Jesus* (Routledge, 2018).
38. Eusebius, *The Church History*, translated by Paul L. Maier (Kregel Academic, 2007).
39. Aidan Kimel, "'I See No God up Here': Gagarin and the Invisible Gardener," Eclectic Orthodoxy, August 2, 2020, https://afkimel.wordpress.com/2020/08/02/i-see-no-god-up-here-gagarin-and-the-invisible-gardener/.
40. Lewis, *Mere Christianity*, book 2, chapter 3.
41. Gary R. Habermas and Michael R. Licona, *The Case for the Resurrection of Jesus* (Kregel Publications, 2004), 49–62.
42. Lewis, *Mere Christianity*, book 2, chapter 3.
43. Peter W. Stoner, *Science Speaks: An Evaluation of Certain Christian Evidences* (Moody Press, 1963), chapter 3.
44. In the Talmud (a source of Jewish tradition), it says, "The whole strength of the mourning is not till the third day; for three days long the soul returns to the grave, thinking that it will return (into the body); when however it sees that the color of its face has changed then it goes away and leaves it" (*Genesis Rabbah,* 100 [64a]).
45. Neil S. Bowers, "An Empty Tomb Is a Beautiful Thing," Wesleyan Church, September 8, 2016, https://www.wesleyan.org/an-empty-tomb-is-a-beautiful-thing-5451.
46. George Lucas, interview in *Time*, April 26, 1999, as cited in Sean McDowell, "Do All Roads Lead to God," Every Student Every School, https://www.everyschool.com/resource/do-all-roads-lead-to-god/.
47. Lee Strobel, "Four Compelling Reasons to Believe the Resurrection Actually Happened," *Relevant*, April 18, 2025, https://relevantmagazine.com/current/lee-strobel-4-compelling-reasons-believe-resurrection-actually-happened/.
48. Rereading the Rabbis; A Woman's Voice, 9 Testimony, Sefaria Library, https://www.sefaria.org/Rereading_the_Rabbis%3B_A_Woman's_Voice%2C_9_Testimony?lang=bi.
49. Ryan Nelson, "How Did the Apostles Die? What We Actually Know," Overview Bible, December 17, 2019, https://overviewbible.com/how-did-the-apostles-die/.
50. Carson, *The Expositor's Bible Commentary*, volume 9, "Matthew," 655.
51. Carson, *The Expositor's Bible Commentary*, volume 9, "Matthew," 661.
52. While the exact source of this quote attributed to Mark Twain is difficult to pinpoint, it reflects what scholars know about his characteristic skepticism and humor about religion hypocrisy.
53. Francis Collins, Veritas Forum, The University of California, Berkeley, February 4, 2008, https://speakola.com/ideas/francis-collins-veritas-forum-berkeley-2008.
54. Francis Collins, "The 'Evidence for Belief': An Interview with Francis Collins," interview by Tom Rosentiel, Pew Research Center, April 17, 2008, https://www.pewresearch.org/science/2008/04/17/the-evidence-for-belief-an-interview-with-francis-collins/.

ABOUT CLIFFE & STUART KNECHTLE

Cliffe Knechtle is senior pastor at Grace Community Church in New Canaan, Connecticut, and host and founder of Give Me an Answer, a university campus ministry that began in 1991 and has since reached tens of millions of Americans via social media. Cliffe loves to converse with skeptics and truth-seekers at universities around the United States, including Harvard, MIT, UCLA, and Stanford.

Stuart Knechtle is a social media influencer who grew Give Me an Answer from a following of roughly 10,000 to now almost 3.5 million followers. He currently debates on university campuses with his father and also goes on popular podcasts for interviews and debates.

From the Publisher

GREAT STUDIES

ARE EVEN BETTER WHEN THEY'RE SHARED!

Help others find this study:

- Post a review at your favorite online bookseller.
- Post a picture on a social media account and share why you enjoyed it.
- Send a note to a friend who would also love it—or, better yet, go through it with them!

Thanks for helping others grow their faith!